DISPENSATIONALISM
Lewis Sperry Chafer

Dispensationalism
Lewis Sperry Chafer (1871-1952)

Exegetica Publishing, Fort Worth, TX, 2015
ISBN: 978-0-9765930-7-2

TABLE OF CONTENTS

Author's Note

The title of this thesis has been chosen reluctantly. It is not intended by it to imply that those who hold what are here set forth as dispensational beliefs are abnormal or disproportionate in doctrine. This thesis purports to demonstrate that so-called dispensationalists find the specific meaning of the Scriptures which God intended to impart and are therefore, by the most exacting proofs, found to be both reasonable and normal in their interpretations. This title is used only that this discussion may be identified in its relation to various articles others have written on this theme.

Much Scripture is cited. Usually the citation is not exhaustive, but serves only to provide one proof-text out of the many. For want of space, the Scriptures could not be quoted. The sincere reader is requested to look up each passage. Otherwise, the value of this thesis, such as it is, will not be gained. This is the second reprint of an article published in Bibliotheca Sacra (XCIII, 390-449.).

Chapter I
Introduction
to
Dispensationalism

<u>Dispensation</u> (noun)

1. The act of dispensing or giving out; distribution; apportionment.

2. Something that is dispensed or given out.

3. A specific arrangement or system by which something is dispensed or administered.

4. Any exemption or release from an obligation or rule, granted by or as if by an authority.

5.   a. An exemption from a church law, a vow, or other similar obligation granted in a particular case by an ecclesiastical authority.
     b. The document containing this exemption.

6. (Theology)
   a. The divine ordering of worldly affairs.
   b. A religious system or code of commands considered to have been divinely revealed or appointed:
     (i.e. "the Moslem dispensation")

<u>Dispensational</u> (adjective)
<u>Dispensatory</u> (adjective) Of, or pertaining to, or granted by dispensation
    → (noun) plural: dispensatories

<u>Dispense</u> (verb)

transitive

("Queen Alexandria dispensed carrots to the thoroughbred from a basket." (Duke of Windsor))

1. To deal out or distribute in parts or portions.
2. To prepare and give out (medicines).
3. To administer (laws, for example).
4. To exempt or release, as from a duty or religious obligation.

intransitive

To grant dispensation or exemption.

<u>Dispenser</u> (noun)

One that dispenses or gives out.

Chapter I
Introduction to Dispensationalism

I. The Word "Dispensation"

A controversy among orthodox theologians over dispensational distinctions is not new. Jonathan Edwards (1703-1758) wrote: "There is, perhaps, no part of divinity attended with so much intricacy, and wherein orthodox divines so much differ as the stating of the precise agreement and difference between the two dispensations of Moses and Christ" (Edward's Works, I, 100). But this discussion, as is often the case, has suffered much for want of definition. abrogate - to abolish or annul by authority; syn: to nullify

The word dispensation is twofold in its import: (1) It may refer to a dispensing or an administration or (2) to an abrogation of standards or existing laws -- such are the dispensations practiced by the Church of Rome. It is obvious that the controversy among theologians is concerned only with the former. The word dispensation is Latin in its origin, being derived from dispensation -- economical management or superintendence -- and has its equivalent in the Greek *oikonomia*, meaning, in this specific usage, 'stewardship' or 'economy' as to special features of divine government in the various ages. To quote the Century Dictionary bearing on the theological import of the word:

(a) The method or scheme by which God has at different times developed his purpose, and revealed himself to man; or the body of privileges bestowed, and duties and responsibilities enjoined, in connection with that scheme or method of revelation: as the Old or Jewish dispensation; the New Gospel dispensation. (b) A period marked by a particular development of the divine purpose and revelation: as the patriarchal dispensation (lasting from Adam to Moses); the Mosaic dispensation (from Moses to Christ); the Christian dispensation.

The Century Dictionary also quotes one pertinent sentence from Bibliotheca Sacra of sixty-two years ago: "The limits of certain dispensational periods were revealed in Scripture" (XLV, 237). In the light of this material, the definition advanced by the late Dr. C.I. Scofield (Scofield Reference Bible, p. 5), namely, "A dispensation is a period of time during which man is tested in respect of obedience to some specific revelation of the will of God," is hardly entitled to the criticism which is aimed against it.

What men, then, according to these definitions, should be classed as dispensationalists? The answer to this question might be stated in a variety of ways. Three of these may suffice: (1) Any person is a dispensationalist who trusts the blood of Christ rather than bringing an animal sacrifice. (2) Any person is a dispensationalist who disclaims any right or title to the land which God covenanted to Israel for an everlasting inheritance. And (3) any person is a dispensationalist who observes the first day of the week rather than the seventh. To all this it would be replied that every Christian does these things, which is obviously true; and it is equally true that, to a very considerable degree, all Christians are dispensationalists.

However, not all Christians, though sincere, are as well instructed in the spiritual content of the Scriptures as others, nor have they seen the necessity of recognizing other and deeper distinctions which do confront the careful student of the Word of God. It should be observed, however, that, apart from extremists who are not now under consideration and mere echo men who appear on either side of a controversy and who have not thought through the problems of interpretation, the instructed dispensationalists of all generations have had as good reason for the distinctions they have made as any Christian might present for trusting only in the blood of Christ apart from all Jewish sacrifices.

The worthy dispensationalist does not create problems of interpretation; he rather seeks to solve the problems which penetrating study of the text of Scripture imposes. Naturally, to the person who has confronted no problems, the work of the advanced student seems divisive and superimposed. Such misunderstandings obtain in every field of human investigation.

II. Misleading Apprehensions

Four misleading apprehensions have been expressed recently by partial dispensationalists. A brief consideration of these statements will be made before turning to the constructive message of this thesis.

1. The term modern dispensationalism implies that dispensationalism is modern. In the recovery of vital truth in the Reformation, dispensational distinctions, like various other doctrines, were not emphasized. The truths thus neglected in the Reformation have since been set forth by devout Bible students, but against the opposition of those who assume that the Reformation secured all that is germane to Systematic Theology.

The testimony, already cited, of Jonathan Edwards (1703-1758) that in his day dispensational distinctions were a living topic of theological discussion indicates the fact that these themes were dominant nearly three hundred years ago. Similarly, a worthy and scholarly research of the Bible with dispensational distinctions in view was made during the last century in England by J.N. Darby, Charles H. Mackintosh, William Kelly, F.W. Grant, and others who developed what is known as the Plymouth Brethren movement. These men created an extensive literature of surpassing value which is strictly Biblical and dispensational, though this literature has been strangely neglected by many conservative theologians. The term anno Domini is intensely dispensational in itself and the familiar dictum attributed to Augustine (354-430, A.D.), "Distinguish the ages and the Scriptures harmonize," could hardly be considered modern.

Until the distortive spiritualizing method of interpretation was introduced by the scholars of the Alexandrian School there was no formulated opposition to the simple belief in and understanding of all that the Sacred Text implies. Abundant evidence for this statement may be drawn from the works of the early fathers, even going back to the Didache, which evidence establishes the fact that Chiliasm, with those dispensational divisions which belong to it, was the orthodox faith of the early church and was far from the heresy that some writers represent it to have been.

2. It has been claimed that dispensationalism is in some respects "illogical" and "leads to disastrous consequences." No argument against this claim need be advanced here other than to point out that dispensationalism has now become one of the most firmly established features of Christian education and is the acknowledged source of untold blessings as well as the inspiration to sacrificial service to uncounted multitudes who testify that the Bible became a new and transforming message to them when dispensational distinctions were observed.

Like the controversy between Arminianism and Calvinism wherein a very great company have been won from Arminianism to Calvinism and few if any from Calvinism to Arminianism, so of the vast company who have turned to dispensationalism very few are known to have ever abandoned the new ground they have taken. It is the dispensationalists who are promoting Bible study movements over the whole land and they are the major factor in all evangelistic and missionary activity today. Dispensationalism has always been disastrous to theological dicta that cannot stand the acid test of Biblical proof.

3. Another claim has been made in recent discussions: "I am a premillennialist, but not a dispensationalist." This

statement evidently supposes that premillennialism is a belief in an event which is isolated from all that precedes and all that follows it. The term premillennial conveys the thought that Christ comes before the millennium. In reality premillennialism becomes a dominating feature of interpretation since it bears on the whole divine program from its beginning to its end. As well might it be argued that though the sun rises in the morning it will neither be preceded by darkness nor accompanied by light as to contend that Christ will come to the earth again, as the Scriptures relate that coming to all that precedes it and all that follows, without causing the most stupendous dispensational changes.

4. And, finally, it has been contended of late that dispensationalism is a modern heretical departure from sound interpretation of the Scriptures, and that the scholarly research of dispensationalists (who of all men are most faithful defenders of every cardinal doctrine of the Word of God) should be classified as a form of Higher Criticism. To quote: "Dispensationalism shares with Higher Criticism its fundamental error." And, again, "In a word, despite all their differences, Higher Criticism and Dispensationalism are in this one respect strikingly similar. Higher Criticism divides the Scriptures up into Documents which differ from or contradict one another. Dispensationalists divide the Bible up into dispensations which differ from and even contradict one another; and so radical is this difference as viewed by the extremist that the Christian of today who accepts the Dispensational views finds his Bible (the part directly intended for him)

shrunk to the compass of the Imprisonment Epistles" ("Modern Dispensationalism," by Oswald T. Allis, former professor of Hebrew in Westminster Theological Seminary, Philadelphia, Evangelical Quarterly, Edinburgh, Scotland, Vol. VIII, No. 1, p. 24).

Though somewhat involved in his expression at the end of this quotation, the author believes Dr. Allis is referring only to extreme dispensationalists of which class there are but very few today. He must know that the great expositors of this and past generations are and were dispensationalists, and that the above description could in no case apply to them. However, the object in view in bringing forward this quotation is the more serious and intended assertion that "Dispensationalism shares with Higher Criticism its fundamental error."

What, then, is this fundamental error to which Dr. Allis refers? It consists, evidently, in the recognition of certain divisions of truth. But Dr. Allis, in common with all Bible students, recognizes some divisions in the Word of God. Thus this "fundamental error" consists in the recognition of distinctions which go beyond Dr. Allis' own conceptions. This point is not stressed to embarrass Dr. Allis, but only that this problem may be reduced to its actual dimensions.

We believe that a partial dispensationalist has a valid reason for the divisions he accepts, and so has the dispensationalist. And the latter will contend that his reasons for these distinctions which go beyond the range of those of the partial dispensationalist are, to him, just as impelling as are the reasons which support the distinctions which he holds in common with the partial dispensationalist. The dispensationalist's larger view of the structure of the Bible is not due to ignorance, lack of logic, or lack of devotion to the integrity of the Scriptures. To hold to the precise character of the Davidic Covenant is no more "divisive" or akin to Higher Criticism than to hold to the precise character of any other covenant. The instructed dispensationalist holds to both.

Beyond this extended introductory word, it is not the purpose of this article to be negatively controversial, though some opposing statements must be considered. In the limited space available it is purposed to make a constructive statement bearing on conservative dispensationalism. In presenting an outline of dispensational fundamentals, proof for statements made will be drawn from the Word of God. Believing the Scriptures of the Old and New Testaments to be the only infallible rule of faith and practice, no appeal is to be made to the creeds, confessions, or doctrinal standards which men have formed.

Recent articles published in defense of sound doctrine have quoted the Westminster Confession for authoritative evidence as much as or more than the Word of God. Men are branded as heterodox who disagree at any point with this Confession. Having declared in ordination vows that he believes the Bible to be the only infallible rule of faith and practice, how can a minister go on to assign infallibility to the Westminster Confession? And if the Westminster Confession is accepted as fallible, could that acceptance be interpreted as being any more than one of general agreement? Even the drafters of the Westminster Confession did not expect their statement to supplant the

Scriptures. They wrote: "The authority of the Holy Scriptures; for which it ought to be believed and obeyed, dependeth not upon the testimony of any man or church, but wholly upon God (who is truth itself), the Author, and therefore it is to be received because it is the Word of God."

Indeed, it is not a long step from the Protestant claim that a man is heretical who does not accept *in toto* some dictum of the Protestant Church to the imposition of Rome which is to the effect that the dogmas of the church are equal in authority with the Scriptures. The theologian who draws his proof as much from the standards of his church as from the Bible is slipping from the true Protestant position. To a student whose conception of doctrine is gained from firsthand searching of the Scriptures, the confessions or creeds, though appreciated for what they contain, are nevertheless characterized by what they do not contain.

An overweening devotion to creedal statements may easily lead to a neglect of much important truth which is outside the range of those creeds.

When good men disagree about doctrine it is usually due to a fundamental difference in premise. Perfect logic, when built on divergent premises, will usually result in irreconcilable conclusions. The controversy between partial dispensationalists and dispensationalists is due to a wide difference in premise. This difference cannot be stated apart from an extended preliminary analysis.

Chapter II
The Creatures of God
Viewed Dispensationally

22   Lewis Sperry Chafer

ANGELS ARE CREATED BEINGS.

Psalm 148: 2, 5, 6   2 Praise ye [the LORD], all his angels: praise ye him, all his hosts. 5 Let them praise the name of the LORD: for he commanded, and they were created. 6 He hath also stablished them for ever and ever: he hath made a decree which shall not pass.
[them - all the LORD's angels, all his hosts (verse 2), the sun & moon & stars (verse 3), the heavens of heavens & the waters that be above the heavens (verse 4)]

Colossians 1:16   For by him (the Father's dear Son, verses 12-15) were all [things] created, that are in heaven, and that are in earth, visible and invisible, whether [they be] thrones, or dominions, or principalities, or powers: all [things] were created by him, and for him.

ANGELS' ABODE IS IN HEAVEN.

Matthew 24:36   But of that day and hour knoweth no man, no, not the angels of heaven, but my Father only.

ANGELS' ACTIVITY IS BOTH ON EARTH AND IN HEAVEN.

Chapter II
The Creatures of God
Viewed Dispensationally

The Bible is God's one and only Book. In it He discloses facts of eternity as well as of time, of heaven and hell as well as of earth, of Himself as well as of His creatures, and of His purposes in all creation. The reader of the Scriptures should be prepared to discover revelation which at times deals with other beings and their destiny quite apart from himself. The Bible presents the origin, present estate, and destiny of four major classes of rational beings in the universe: the angels, the Gentiles, the Jews, and the Christians. Nothing could be more germane to true Biblical interpretation than the observance of this fact that these divisions of rational beings continue what they are throughout their history. The revealed divine program for each of these groups will here be traced in brief.

(adj.) germane : Having a significant bearing upon a point at hand; related; sym. relevant   pertinent.

I. The Angels

The angels are created beings (Ps. 148:2, 5; Col. 1:16), their abode is in heaven (Matt. 24:36), their activity is both on earth and in heaven (Ps. 103:20; Luke 15:10; Heb. 1:14), and their destiny is in the celestial city (Heb. 12:22; Rev. 21:12). They remain angels throughout their existence.

They neither propagate nor do they die. There is no reason for confusing the angels with any other creatures in God's universe. Even though they fall, as in the case of Satan and the demons, they are still classed as angels (Matt. 25:41).

II. The Gentiles

In regard to their racial stock, the Gentiles had their origin in Adam and their natural headship is in him. They have partaken of the fall, and, though they are the subjects of prophecy which predicts that some of them will yet share, as a subordinate people, with Israel in her coming kingdom glory (Isa. 2:4; 14:1-2; 60:3, 5, 12; 62:2; Matt. 25:34; Acts 15:17), they, with respect to their estate in the period from Adam to Christ, are under a fivefold indictment, namely, "without Christ, being aliens from the commonwealth of Israel, and strangers from the covenants of promise, having no hope, and without God in the world" (Eph. 2:12).

With the death, resurrection, and ascension of Christ, and the descent of the Spirit, the door of gospel privilege was opened unto the Gentiles (Acts 10:45; 11:17-18; 13:47-48), and out of them God is now calling an elect company (Acts 15:14). Their new proffered blessings in this age do not consist in being permitted to share in Israel's earthly covenants, which even Israel is not now enjoying; but rather, through riches of grace in Christ Jesus, they are privileged to be partakers of a heavenly citizenship and glory. It is revealed that the mass of Gentiles will not in this age enter by faith into these heavenly riches.

Therefore, this people, designated as "the nations," go on, and at the end of their stewardship as earth-rulers, which is the termination of "the times of the Gentiles"

(Luke 21:24; cf. Dan. 2:36-44), they of that generation will, at the end of the tribulation period (cf. Matt. 24:8-31 with 25:31-46), be called upon to stand before the Messiah King, seated on the throne of His glory (Matt. 25:31-32) here on the earth. At that time, some who are found on the left and who are designated "the goats" will be dismissed into "everlasting fire, prepared for the devil and his angels," but those who are found on His right, who are designated as "sheep," will be ushered into "the kingdom" prepared for them from the foundation of the world (Matt. 25:31-46).

The basis of this judgment and its disposition of each of these groups, who together represent the sum total of that generation of the Gentile nations, will be meritorious to the last degree. The "sheep" enter the kingdom and the "goats" the lake of fire on the sole issue of their treatment of a third group whom Christ designates "my brethren." This context does not bear out the interpretation that this is a description of a last and final judgment when all saved people of all the ages are ushered into heaven; for the saved, each and every one, when departing this world are immediately present with the Lord in heaven (Acts 7:55-56; 2 Cor. 5:8; Phil. 1:23); and who, according to such an interpretation, would answer to "my brethren"? The scene is at the close of the great tribulation (Matt. 24:21) after the removal of the Church from the earth, and at a time when nations will be divided over the Semitic question.

The issue is one regarding what nations will be chosen to enter Israel's Messianic kingdom on the earth. The destiny of the Gentiles is further revealed when it is declared concerning the city which, after the creation of the new heavens and the new earth, comes down from God out of heaven (Rev. 3:12; 21:2, 10), that "the nations of them which are saved shall walk in the light of it: and the kings of the earth do bring their glory and honour into it. ... And they shall bring the glory and honour of the nations into it" (Rev. 21:24-26). The term "the nations of them which are saved" could not refer to the Church for her destiny is not earthly, neither is she ever termed "the nations," nor does she include the kings of the earth in her number.

In this same context, the city itself is said to be "the bride, the Lamb's wife," which is the Church (Rev. 21:2, 9-10). Thus it is disclosed that -- in spite of the fact that a dispensation of world-rule is committed unto them, that in this age the gospel is preached unto them with its offers of heavenly glory, that in the coming age they share the blessings of the kingdom with Israel, and that they appear in the future ages -- they remain Gentiles, in contradistinction to the one nation Israel, to the end of the picture; and there is no defensible ground for diverting or misapplying this great body of Scripture bearing on the Gentiles.

III. The Jews

Whatever Abraham was nationally before he was called of God, it is certain that God set him apart and through him secured a race so distinct in its individuality that from the time of the Exodus to the end of the record of their history they are held as antipodal of all other nations combined. Whatever Abraham's distinctive physical characteristics may have been, it is undeniable that his spiritual characteristics were far removed from those of the idolatrous heathen among whom he was reared, and the race which sprang from him through Isaac and Jacob has ever been unique both with regard to spiritual values and physical appearance.

Following the first eleven chapters of Genesis wherein the first third of human history is recorded and which concern a period of two thousand years when there was but one division of the human family on the earth, the record enters upon the second third of human history which period of two thousand years extends from Abraham to Christ. In a usual edition of the Bible totaling 1,351 pages, 1,132 bear almost exclusively upon this second period, and concern the physical seed of Abraham through Isaac and Jacob. During this extended period there are two divisions of humanity on the earth, but the Gentile is then considered only in the light of his relation to Israel. Israel is set apart as an elect nation. Her specific divine favors are enumerated thus: "Who are Israelites; to whom pertaineth the adoption, and the glory, and the covenants, and the giving of the law, and the service of God, and the promises; whose are the fathers, and of whom as concerning the flesh Christ came, who is over all, God blessed for ever. Amen" (Rom. 9:4-5).

Out of the covenants Jehovah has made with Israel, five eternal features are dominant -- a national entity (Jer. 31:36), a land in perpetuity (Gen. 13:15), a throne (2 Sam. 7:16; Ps. 89:36), a king (Jer. 33:21), and a kingdom (Dan. 7:14). Though Jehovah reserves the right to chasten even to the extent of scattering His people through all the nations, their land being trodden down of Gentiles and their throne vacant for a time, yet His eternal purposes cannot fail. This people are to be regathered and the land will be possessed forever (Deut. 30:1-6; Jer. 23:5-8; Ezek. 37:21-25). Their rightful King, the Son of David, will occupy the Davidic throne forever (Ps. 89:34-37; Isa. 9:6-7; Jer. 33:17; Luke 1:31-33; Rev. 11:15). Each of the two major passages on the virgin birth of Christ -- one in the Old Testament (Isa. 7:14 with 9:6-7) and one in the New Testament (Luke 1:31-33) -- record the prediction, in addition to the virgin birth, that Christ will occupy the Davidic throne forever.

According to very much prophecy, the anticipated Messiah would come as a resistless Lion and as a sacrificial Lamb. Peter testifies to the perplexity of the prophets over this seeming paradox (1 Pet. 1:10-11). Isaiah blends the events connected with the two advents into one vast, all-inclusive expectation (Isa. 61:1-5); and even the angel Gabriel was not permitted to disclose the fact of two advents separated by the present age, but refers to the events of both advents as though they belonged to one uninterrupted program (Luke 1:31-33). However, to David were given two important revelations, namely, (a) that God's eternal Son would die a sacrificial death (Ps. 22:1-21; 69:20-21), and (b) that He would occupy David's throne forever (2 Sam. 7:16-29; Ps. 89:34-37). David reasoned that if all this were true, God's Son must first die and be raised again from the dead and thus be free to reign forever.

This conclusion on the part of David was one of the most vital features of Peter's Pentecostal sermon (Acts 2:25-36), in which he is proving that the Lord Jesus is, in spite of His death, the eternal Messiah to Israel. Thus it was disclosed that the Son of David would first die and then be raised again, that the Davidic promise of an eternal occupant of David's throne might be fulfilled. However, it was as definitely predicted that Christ would at His first advent offer Himself to Israel as their King, not in the role of a resistless conquering monarch, as He will yet come (Rev. 19:15-16), but "meek" and "lowly" (Zech. 9:9; cf. Matt. 21:5). Yet, in spite of prediction that Christ would make a precross offer of Himself to Israel as their King, coming in "lowly guise," Dr. Allis in his article on "Modern Dispensationalism" (quoted above) refers to the belief which dispensationalists hold -- that Christ offered the kingdom to Israel and that it was rejected and postponed -- as a theory characterized by intricacies and impossible. He states that this theory seriously minimizes "the value and centrality of the Cross in Biblical Revelation" (Ibid., p. 34).

Likewise, a Presbyterian minister of the south has written an article which has been published by a reputable Presbyterian journal also accusing the late Dr. C.I. Scofield of modernistic teaching because he seemed to minimize the cross by his advocacy of the theory that the kingdom was offered to Israel before the death of Christ. These men are Calvinists, yet they are disturbed over the seeming conflict between divine sovereignty and human will. If the ground of their objection to the "postponement theory" stands, then there was no assurance that there would be a Jewish nation until Abraham made his decision to obey God; there was no certainty that Christ would be born until Mary gave her consent; there was no assurance that Christ would die until Pilate so ordered.

In the light of two determining facts, namely, (a) that Jehovah's Lamb was in the redeeming purpose slain from the foundation of the world and (b) that had Adam not sinned there could have been no need of a redeemer, why did Jehovah tell Adam not to sin? And what would have become of the redemptive purpose had Adam obeyed God? These objections to the so-called postponement theory do not take into consideration the fact of the divinely purposed test involved and the necessary postponement resulting from the failure under testing, the failure itself being anticipated. These are evidently very serious problems for some Calvinists to face. If it be claimed that the birth and death of Christ were predicted and therefore made sure, it is equally true that the precross offer of the earthly Messianic kingdom to Israel by her Messiah in the days of His "lowly guise" was also made sure by prediction.

It is equally made sure by prediction that Christ would be crucified, which was Israel's official rejection of their King (Ps. 118:22-24 with 1 Pet. 2:6-8; Matt. 21:42-45; Luke 19:14, 27; Acts 4:10-12), be raised from the dead (Ps. 16:8-10), and ultimately sit on David's earthly throne and reign over the house of Jacob forever (Isa. 9:6-7; Matt. 2:6; Luke 1:31-33). The prophet declared of Christ that He would be "despised and rejected of men," and John states, "He came unto his own, but his own [Israel] received Him not" (John 1:11).

The truth set forth in this last passage is of utmost importance. The "rejection" on the part of the nation Israel was not the personal rejection of a crucified and risen Savior as He is now rejected when the gospel is refused. It was a nation to whom a Messiah King was promised, rejecting their King. They did not say, "We will not believe on this Savior for the saving of our souls"; but they did say in effect, "We will not have this man to reign over us." This distinction is important since it determines the precise character of their sin.

Two years after their departure from Egypt, God offered to Israel an entrance into their land at Kadesh-Barnea. They rejected the offer. God knew they would reject it, yet it was a bona fide offer He made to them. Yea, it was in the divine counsel that they would reject, become guilty of that specific sin, and, as a punishment, be returned to thirty-eight more years of wilderness experience. After that, they were taken into the land by His sovereign hand without a question concerning their own wishes. Since He had worked in their hearts to do His good pleasure, they went in with songs of rejoicing. This history is allegorical, if not typical. The two years of wilderness experience preceding the offer at Kadesh are typical of the six hundred years Israel had been out of their kingdom when Christ came. The rejection of the divine offer at Kadesh is typical of the rejection of Christ.

A possible entrance into the land at Kadesh was a bona fide offer to Israel made by Jehovah in the full knowledge that they would reject it, and in spite of the fact that His eternal purpose required them to reject the offer and return to thirty-eight more years of trial. Had the salvation of the world hung on the added years of trial after Kadesh, hesitating Calvinists would shrink back from admitting that the Kadesh offer was ever made, or, if made, was genuine. All would be branded as a theory characterized by intricacies and impossible. The added thirty-eight years are typical of Israel's present condition as a people yet deprived of their land and the blessings of their covenants. The entrance of Israel into the land by sovereign power corresponds to the final restoration of that nation to their inheritance which Jehovah covenanted to them as an everlasting possession (Gen. 13:14-17). That Israel will yet be regathered into her own land is the burden of about twenty Old Testament predictions beginning with Deuteronomy 30:3.

The death of Christ is neither incidental, accidental, nor fortuitous. It is the central truth of the Bible and the central fact of the universe. It was also in the purpose of God that Christ's death should be accomplished by Israel as their act of rejecting their King. It is also true that they did not and could not reject what was not first offered to them. In the present unforeseen age -- which is bounded by the two advents of Christ and often termed parenthetical or an intercalation in the sense that it is unforeseen in the divine program for the Jews as reflected in the prophecies concerning them and is not accounted for in the Gentile program of successive monarchies symbolized by the colossal image of Nebuchadnezzar's dream -- the Jews, like the Gentiles, are, as individuals, shut up at the present time to the message of the gospel of saving grace through faith in Christ.

The agelong Jewish advantage because of divine election is, for an age, set aside and the Apostle declares, "There is no difference." They are as individuals alike with the Gentiles "under sin" (Rom. 3:9), and as individuals alike with the Gentiles in that God is rich in mercy to all that call upon Him (Rom. 10:12). This is a new message to Gentiles and equally new to Jews. The divine favor proffered to Gentiles does not consist in offering them a share in the national blessings of Israel, nor does it provide a way whereby the Jew may realize the specific features of his national covenants. Though present salvation is into the kingdom of God (John 3:3), no earthly kingdom is now being offered to any people. Colossians 1:13 is no exception. Should the present king of Great Britain marry a woman of another nation he would bring her into his kingdom, not as a subject, but as a consort. The present divine purpose is the outcalling from both Jews and Gentiles of that company who are the Bride of Christ, who are, therefore, every one to partake of His standing, being in Him, to be like Him, and to reign with Him on the earth (Rev. 20:4, 6; 22:5). To the nation Israel Christ is Messiah, Emmanuel, and King; to the Church He is Head, Bridegroom, and Lord, the last designation connoting His sovereign authority over the Church. These statements, admittedly dogmatic, are easily verified.

At the end of this age, Israel must pass through the great tribulation, which is specifically characterized as "the time of Jacob's trouble" (Jer. 30:4-7; Dan. 12:1; Matt. 24:21); and, before entering her kingdom, she must come before her King in judgment. Of this event Ezekiel writes: "I will bring you out from the people, and will gather you out of the countries wherein ye are scattered. ... And I will cause you to pass under the rod, and I will bring you into the bond of the covenant: and I will purge out from among you the rebels, and them that transgress against me" (Ezek. 20:34-38. The entire context should be considered, 33-44. Cf., also, Isa. 1:24-26; Ps. 50:1-7; Mal. 3:2-5; 4:1-2). Israel's judgments are likewise described by Christ in Matthew 24:15-25:30. That this Scripture refers to Israel is certain from the fact that the Church does not come into judgment (John 3:18; 5:24; Rom. 8:1, A.R.V., 38-39), and that the description of the judgment of the nations does not begin until verse 31. It therefore follows that Israel's judgments are in view in the passage in question. The incomparable tribulation is ended by the glorious return of Christ to the earth (Ps. 2:1-9; Isa. 63:1-6; Matt. 24:27-31; 2 Thess. 2:3-12; Rev. 19:11-21); Israel's judgments, according to the context of Matthew 24:30-25:30, follow the glorious appearing of Christ; and the judgment of the nations occurs when He is seated on the throne of His glory (Matt. 25:31-32).

The Day of Jehovah, which extended period occupies so large a part of Old Testament prophecy, begins with the judgments of Jehovah in the earth, mentioned in the foregoing, and continues on including the return of Christ to the earth and all the millennial glory for Israel and the Gentiles. Zechariah 14:1-21 predicts the beginning of that long period, while 2 Peter 3:4-15 (note, in this connection, Peter declares "one day is with the Lord as a thousand years, and a thousand years as one day") and Revelation 20:7-15 describe the end of that period. The whole extended "day" is characterized by the presence of Christ reigning on the earth with His Bride, by Satan being bound and in the abyss, and by the realization on Israel's part of all the glory and blessedness promised that people in Jehovah's covenants with them.

More space than this thesis may claim would be required to quote even the major prophecies bearing on this theme (cf. Ps. 45:8-17; 72:1-20; Isa. 11:1-12:6; 54:1-55:13; 60:1-66:24; Jer. 23:5-8; 31:1-40; 33:1-26; Ezek. 34:11-31; 36:16-38; 37:1-14; 40:1--48:35; Dan. 2:44-45; 7:13-14; Zech.

14:1-21; Mal. 4:1-6). These promises are all of an earthly glory and concern a land which Jehovah has given as an everlasting possession to His elect people, Israel, to whom He said, "I have loved thee with an everlasting love" (Jer. 31:3). Little consideration, indeed, is given to the confusion or inconsistencies which arise when, under a spiritualizing method of interpretation, these blessings which are addressed to the elect nation and related to their land and King are applied to an elect heavenly people called out from all nations to whom no land has ever been given, and who are not now or at any future time said to be subjects of the King.

There is no scholarly reason for applying the Scriptures which bear upon the past, the present, or the future of Israel to any other people than that nation of whom these Scriptures speak. The real unity of the Bible is preserved only by those who observe with care the divine program for Gentiles, for Jews, and for Christians in their individual and unchanging continuity.

IV. The Christians

The current and last third of human history, extending from the first advent of Christ to the present hour, is characterized by three widely different classes of people dwelling together on the earth. As in the preceding age, all divine purpose centered about the Jew, and the Gentile was in evidence only as he was related to Israel; so in this age the divine purpose centers in the new group which is present, and the Jew and the Gentile are seen only as those to whom the gospel is to be preached alike and from whom this new elect company is being called out by a spiritual birth of each individual who believes to the saving of his soul.

The Scriptures addressed specifically to this company are: the Gospel by John -- especially the Upper Room Discourse, the Acts, and the Epistles. The Synoptic Gospels, though on the surface presenting a simple narrative, are, nevertheless, a field for careful, discriminating study on the part of the true expositor. In these Gospels Christ is seen as loyal to and vindicating the Mosaic Law under which He lived; He also anticipates the kingdom age in connection with the offer of Himself as Israel's King; and, when His rejection is indicated, He announces His death and resurrection and the expectation concerning a heavenly people (Matt. 16:18) for whom He gave Himself in redeeming love (Eph. 5:25-27).

An extensive body of Scripture declares directly or indirectly that the present age is unforeseen and intercalary in its character and in it a new humanity appears on the earth with an incomparable new headship in the resurrected Christ, which company is being formed by the regenerating power of the Spirit. It is likewise revealed that there is now "no difference" between Jews and Gentiles generally, either with respect to their need of salvation (Rom. 3:9) or the specific message to be preached to them (Rom. 10:12). It is seen, also, that in this new body wherein Jews and Gentiles are united by a common salvation, the middle wall of partition -- the agelong enmity between Jew and Gentile -- is broken down, itself having been "slain" by Christ on the cross, thus making peace (Eph. 2:14-18).

In fact, all former distinctions are lost, those thus saved having come upon new ground where there is neither Jew nor Gentile, but where Christ is all in all (Gal. 3:28; Col. 3:11). The New Testament also records that the individual Christian, being indwelt by Christ, now possesses eternal life and its hope of glory (Col. 1:27), and, being in Christ, is enriched with the perfect standing of Christ, since all that Christ is -- even the righteousness of God -- is imputed unto him. The Christian is thus already constituted a heavenly citizen (Phil. 3:20) and, being raised with Christ (Col. 3:1-3), and seated with Him (Eph. 2:6), belongs to another sphere -- so definitely, indeed, that Christ can say of the Christian: "Ye are not of the world, even as I am not of the world" (John 17:14, 16; cf. 15:18-19).

It is likewise to be observed that since this spiritual birth and heavenly position in Christ are supernatural, they are, of necessity, wrought by God alone, and that human cooperation is excluded, the only responsibility imposed on the human side being that of faith which trusts in the only One who is able to save. To this heavenly people, who are the New Creation of God (2 Cor. 5:17; Gal. 6:15), is committed, not in any corporate sense but only as individuals, a twofold responsibility, namely, (a) to adorn by a Christlike life the doctrine which they represent by the very nature of their salvation, and (b) to be His witnesses to the uttermost parts of the earth. It is similarly believed that the Scriptures which direct the Christian in his holy walk and service are adapted to the fact that he is not now striving to secure a standing with God, but is already "accepted in the beloved" (Eph. 1:6), and has attained unto every spiritual blessing (Eph. 1:3; Col. 2:10).

It is evident that no human resource could enable any person to arise to the fulfillment of these heaven-high responsibilities and that God, anticipating the believer's inability to walk worthy of the calling wherewith he is called, has freely bestowed His empowering Spirit to indwell every one who is saved.

Of this same heavenly company it is declared that they, when their elect number is complete, will be removed from this earth. The bodies of those that have died will be raised and living saints will be translated (1 Cor. 15:20-57; 1 Thess. 4:13-17). In glory, the individuals who comprise this company will be judged as regards their rewards for service (1 Cor. 3:9-15; 9:18-27; 2 Cor. 5:10-11), be married to Christ (Rev. 19:7-9), and then return with Him to share as His Consort in His reign (Luke 12:35-36; Jude 1:14-15; Rev. 19:11-16). This New Creation people, like the angels, Israel, and the Gentiles, may be traced on into the eternity to come (Heb. 12:22-24; Rev. 21:1-22:5). But, it will be remembered, the Christian possesses no land (Ex. 20:12; Matt. 5:5); no house (Matt. 23:38; Acts 15:16), though of the household of God; no earthly capital or city (Isa. 2:1-4; Ps. 137:5-6); no earthly throne (Luke 1:31-33); no earthly kingdom (Acts 1:6-7); no king to whom he is subject (Matt. 2:2), though Christians may speak of Christ as "the King" (1 Tim. 1:17; 6:15); and no altar other than the cross of Christ (Heb. 13:10-14).

Chapter III
Scripture Doctrine
Viewed Dispensationally

Chapter III
Scripture Doctrine
Viewed Dispensationally

A true religion consists in a specific relationship, with its corresponding responsibilities, divinely set up between God and man. There is no revelation of any distinctive relation having been set up either between God and the angels or between God and the Gentiles which partakes of the character of a true religion, but God has entered into relation with the Jew, which results in Judaism, or what the Apostle identifies as the religion of the Jews (Acts 26:5; Gal. 1:13; cf. James 1:26-27), and with the Christian, which results in Christianity, or what the New Testament writers designate as "the faith" (Jude 1:3) and "this way" (Acts 9:2; 22:4; cf. 18:26; 2 Pet. 2:2).

Judaism and Christianity have much in common; each is ordained of God to serve a specific purpose. They incorporate similar features -- God, man, righteousness, sin, redemption, salvation, human responsibility, and human destiny -- but these similarities do not establish identity since the dissimilarities far outnumber the similarities. There are remarkable points of likeness between the laws of Great Britain and the laws of the

United States, but this fact does not constitute these two nations one.

A complete religious system provides at least seven distinctive features, all of which are present both in Judaism and in Christianity. These features are: (1) an acceptable standing on the part of man before God; (2) a manner of life consistent with that standing; (3) a divinely appointed service; (4) a righteous ground whereon God may graciously forgive and cleanse the erring; (5) a clear revelation of the responsibility on the human side upon which divine forgiveness and cleansing may be secured; (6) an effective basis upon which God may be worshiped and petitioned in prayer; and (7) a future hope.

It should be observed that though Judaism and Christianity have much in common, they never merge the one into the other. Having each its own eschatology reaching on into eternity, any attempt to fuse these two systems in the interests of a mere idealistic unity of the Scriptures is doomed to fail under the acid test of an unprejudiced, faithful searching of the Word of God. A constructive work on the eschatology of Judaism, such as an Old Testament scholar of the standing of Dr. Allis might produce, is a desideratum. It should go beyond the bounds of the Westminster Confession, which is itself greatly restricted in its eschatology. Equally to be desired is an exhaustive work on the soteriology of Judaism; observing in it the first law of a true Old Testament Theology, namely, that in every instance its doctrine shall stand only on the body of truth which obtained in the period under consideration.

The all-too-common practice of imposing Christianity back upon Judaism or Judaism forward upon Christianity, is the cause of that dire confusion which appears in some theological literature. The Word of God distinguishes between earth and heaven, even after they are created new. Similarly and as clearly it distinguishes between God's consistent and eternal earthly purpose, which is the substance of Judaism; and His consistent and eternal heavenly purpose which is the substance of Christianity, and it is as illogical and fanciful to contend that Judaism and Christianity ever merge as it would be to contend that heaven and earth cease to exist as separate spheres. Dispensationalism has its foundation in and is understood in the distinction between Judaism and Christianity.

I. An Acceptable Standing on the Part of Man Before God

Whatever may have been the divine method of dealing with individuals before the call of Abraham and the giving of the law by Moses, it is evident that, with the call of Abraham and the giving of the law and all that has followed, there are two widely different, standardized, divine provisions, whereby man, who is utterly fallen, might stand in the favor of God, namely, (a) by physical birth into Judaism or (b) by spiritual birth into Christianity or the kingdom of God.

1. Divine Grace Upon Israel.

Apart from the privilege accorded proselytes of joining the congregation of Israel -- which seemed to bear little fruitage -- entrance into the right to share in the covenants of blessing designed for the earthly people was and is by physical birth. It was no vain boast when the Apostle declared of himself that he was "of the stock of Israel" (Phil. 3:5), nor is there any uncertain generalization in the statement that Christ "was a minister of the circumcision to confirm the promises made unto the fathers" (Rom. 15:8).

The national blessings of Israel are recorded thus: "Who are Israelites; to whom pertaineth the adoption, and the glory, and the covenants, and the giving of the law, and the service of God, and the promises; whose are the fathers, and of whom as concerning the flesh Christ came" (Rom. 9:4-5). Though they went down into Egypt a family, they came out a nation and Jehovah redeemed them as a nation unto Himself both by blood and by power. It was not an individual redemption since it was not restricted to that generation, but Israel remains a redeemed nation throughout all her history (Isa. 63:4). On the human side, the passover lamb saved the physical life of Israel's first-born.

On the divine side, the lamb, as an anticipation of God's perfect Lamb, gave Jehovah freedom to redeem a nation forever. That Israel was already in Jehovah's favor is revealed in Exodus 8:23; 9:6, 26; 10:23. The redeemed nation became Jehovah's abiding treasure (Ex. 19:5; Deut. 4:32-40; Ps. 135:4). What Jehovah has covenanted to His elect nation is one thing, and what He covenants to individuals within that nation is quite another thing. The national entity has been and will be preserved forever according to covenant promise (Isa. 66:22; Jer. 31:35-37; Gen. 17:7-8).

The individual Israelite, on the other hand, was subject to a prescribed and regulated conduct which carried with it a penalty of individual judgment for every failure (Deut. 28:58-62; Ezek. 20:33-44; Matt. 24:51; 25:12, 30). The national standing (but not necessarily the spiritual state) of each Israelite, was secured by physical birth. Some of that nation did by faithfulness attain to more personal blessing than others of the nation (cf. Luke 2:25, 37), and some gloried in their tribal relationship (cf. Phil. 3:5); but these things added nothing to their rights within their covenants, which rights were secured to every one alike by physical birth.

2. Divine Grace Upon Christians.

The heavenly people, whether taken individually from either Jewish or Gentile stock, attain immediately by faith unto a standing as perfect as that of Christ, which standing is secured by a spiritual birth and all the saving operations of God which accompany it. They are individually redeemed by the blood of Christ, born of the Spirit into a relationship in which God becomes their Father and they become His legitimate sons and heirs ·· even joint-heirs with Christ.

Through the regenerating work of the Spirit they have Christ begotten in them (Col. 1:27), and they receive the divine nature which is eternal life (Rom. 6:23). They are forgiven all trespasses to such a degree that they will never come into condemnation (Col. 2:13; John 3:18; Rom. 8:1, A.R.V.), and justified forever (Rom. 3:21-5:11). They died in Christ's death (Rom. 6:1-10), they rose in Christ's resurrection (Col. 3:1-3), and they are seated with Christ in the heavenlies (Eph. 2:6). By the baptizing work of the Spirit they are "joined to the Lord" (Rom. 6:1-7; 1 Cor. 12:13; Gal. 3:27) and, being thus in Christ, their standing before God is no less than the perfection of Christ in whom they are accepted (2 Cor. 5:21; Eph. 1:6). Being in Christ, they are one in each other in a mystic union which is both incomparable and incomprehensible -- a unity like that within the blessed Trinity (John 17:21-23). They are already constituted citizens of heaven (Phil. 3:20). These blessings are not only as exalted and spiritual as heaven itself and eternal, but they are secured apart from all human merit at the instant one believes on Christ to the saving of the soul.

Any Bible student can verify the assertion which is here made that not one of these distinctive characteristics of a Christian, and the list here presented could be greatly extended, is ever said to belong to Israel as such either as individuals or nationally; and almost none of these spiritual blessings are predicated of any individual before the death and resurrection of Christ. The Upper Room Discourse (John 13:1-17:26), though spoken before the death of Christ, is, nevertheless, a record in anticipation of all that would be after His death and even after Pentecost.

II. A Divinely Specified Manner of Life

Quite apart from the revealed will of God as recorded of earlier ages, the Bible sets forth at length three distinct and complete divine rulings which govern human action. None of these rulings are addressed to the angels or to the Gentiles as such. Two are addressed to Israel -- one in the age that is past, known as the Mosaic Law, and the other the setting forth of the terms of admission into, and the required conduct in, the Messianic kingdom when that kingdom is set up in the earth. The third is addressed to Christians and provides divine direction in this age for the heavenly people who are already perfected, with respect to standing, in Christ Jesus. Since the Bible is God's one book for all the ages, it should be no more difficult to recognize its reference to future ages than to recognize its reference to completed past ages.

These three rules of life do present widely different economies. This is evident both from their distinctive characteristics as set forth in the Word of God and from the very nature of the case. Concerning the nature of the case, it may be said that the divine administration in the earth could not be the same after the death of Christ, after His resurrection, after His ascension and the inauguration of His present ministry, after the advent of the Holy Spirit on the Day of Pentecost, and after the ad interim disannulling of Judaism, as it was before those events. Nor could the divine administration be the same after the removal of the Church from the earth, after the regathering of Israel and the restoration of Judaism, after the judgment of the nations, after the binding of Satan, and after the seating of Christ at His second advent on David's throne to rule over the whole earth, as it is now before those events occur.

Since the faith of some cannot be extended to the point of visualizing unfulfilled prophecy into reality, it might be the part of wisdom to restrict this argument to the first group of events, namely, those which form a cleavage between the past age and the present age. Because of the fact that these events are now history (though at one time they were predictive prophecy) their reality is hardly disputed even by the unregenerate man. Nevertheless the second group of events, which separate the present age from the age to come, are the keys to the understanding of God's kingdom purposes in the earth, and without these keys the casual reader is left with little else to do other than to fall in with the Romish fiction of a world-conquering church under a supposed supremacy of an irresistible kingdom of God on the earth.

No doubt will be raised by any intelligent Christian concerning the truth that it is within the range of divine power to transform society in this age, or at any other time. The question is really one of whether world-transformation is the divine purpose for this age; and until the one who believes that this is the divine purpose has made a reasonable exposition and disposition in harmony with his views of the vast body of Scripture that discloses the confusion and wickedness with which this age is said to end, there is little to be gained by accusing those who believe God's present purposes to be the outcalling of the Church of "dishonoring the Spirit of God," or of "minimizing the value of the cross." Especially is such a charge without force when it is known that those so accused believe that all of God's triumph in this and every age will be only by virtue of that cross.

The Mosaic system was designed to govern Israel in the land and was an ad interim form of divine government between that gracious administration, described in Exodus 19:4, and the coming of Christ (John 1:17; Rom. 4:9-16; Gal. 3:19-25). It was in three parts, namely, (a) "the commandments," which governed Israel's moral life (Ex.

20:1-17); (b) "the judgments," which governed Israel's civic life (Ex. 21:1-24:11); and (c) "the ordinances," which governed Israel's religious life (Ex. 24:12-31:18). These provisions were holy, just, and good (Rom. 7:12, 14), but they carried a penalty (Deut. 28:58-62) and, because they were not kept by Israel, they became a "ministration of death" (Rom. 7:10; 2 Cor. 3:7). The law was not of faith, but of works (Gal. 3:12). It was ordained unto life (Rom. 7:10), but because of the weakness of the flesh of those to whom it made its appeal (Rom. 8:3), there was, as a practical result, no law given which could give life (Gal. 3:21).

The law did, however, serve as the *paidagogos*, or child-conductor, to lead to Christ -- both immediately, as Christ was foreshadowed in the sacrifices, and dispen-sationally, as described in Galatians 3:23-25. Though almost every intrinsic value contained in the law system is carried forward and incorporated into the present grace system, it still remains true that the law as an ad interim system did come to its end and a new divine economy superseded it. No more decisive language could be employed on this point than is used in John 1:17; Romans 6:14; 7:2-6; 10:4; 2 Corinthians 3:6-13; Galatians 3:23-25; 5:18. These Scriptures should not be slighted, as they too often are, by those who would impose the law system upon the heavenly people. It is useless to claim that it was the judgments and ordinances that were done away and that the commandments abide, since it is that which was "written and engraven in stones" which is said to have been "done away" and "abolished" (2 Cor. 3:11, 13). Nor is the situation relieved for those who claim that the law has ceased as a means of justification; for it was never that, nor could it be (Gal. 3:11).

The heavenly people, by the very exalted character of their salvation being "made" to stand in all the perfection of Christ (Rom. 3:22; 5:1; 8:1; 10:4; 2 Cor. 5:21; Gal. 3:22; Eph. 1:6), have no burden laid upon them of establishing personal merit before God since they are perfected forever in Christ (Heb. 10:9-14); but they do have the new responsibility of "walking worthy" of their high calling (Rom. 12:1-2; Eph. 4:1-3; Col. 3:1-3). No system of merit, such as was the law, could possibly be applied to a people who by riches of divine grace have attained to a perfect standing, even every spiritual blessing in Christ Jesus (Eph. 1:3; Col. 2:10).

It is to be expected that the injunctions addressed to a perfected heavenly people will be as exalted as heaven itself, and they are (cf. John 13:34; Rom. 6:11-13; 2 Cor. 10:3-5; Gal. 5:16; Eph. 4:30; 5:18). Similarly, as these requirements are superhuman and yet the doing of them is most essential, God has provided that each individual thus saved shall be indwelt by the Holy Spirit to the end that he may, by dependence on the Spirit and by the power of the Spirit, live a supernatural, Godhonoring life ·· not, indeed, to be accepted, but because he is accepted. Those who would intrude the Mosaic system of merit into this heaven-high divine administration of superabounding grace either have no conception of the character of that merit which the law required, or are lacking in the comprehension of the glories of divine grace.

The third administration which is contained in the Bible is that which is designed to govern the earthly people in relation to their coming earthly kingdom. It is explicit, also, with regard to the requirements that are to be imposed upon those who enter that kingdom. This body of Scripture is found in the Old Testament portions which anticipate the Messianic kingdom and in large portions of the Synoptic Gospels. The essential elements of a grace administration -- faith as the sole basis of acceptance with God, unmerited acceptance through a perfect standing in Christ, the present possession of eternal life, an absolute security from all condemnation, and the enabling power of the indwelling Spirit -- are not found in the kingdom administration. On the other hand, it is declared to be the fulfilling of "the law and the prophets" (Matt. 5:17-18; 7:12), and is seen to be an extension of the Mosaic Law into realms of merit-seeking which blast and wither as the Mosaic system could never do (Matt. 5:20-48). These kingdom injunctions, though suited to the conditions that will then obtain, could perfect no one as men in Christ are now perfected, nor are they adapted as a rule of life for those already complete in Christ Jesus.

These systems do set up conflicting and opposing principles; but since these difficulties appear only when an attempt is made to coalesce systems, elements, and principles which God has separated, the conflicts really do not exist at all outside these unwarranted unifying efforts; in fact they rather demonstrate the necessity of a due recognition of all God's different and distinct administrations. The true unity of the Scriptures is not discovered when one blindly seeks to fuse these opposing principles into one system, but rather it is found when God's plain differentiations are observed. The dispensationalist does not create these differences as he is sometimes accused of doing.

The conflicting principles, in the text of Scripture, are observable to all who penetrate deep enough to recognize the essential features of divine administration. Instead of creating the problems, the dispensationalist is the one who has a solution for them. If the ideals of an earthly people for long life in the land which God gave unto them (Ex. 20:12; Ps. 37:3, 11, 34; Matt. 5:5) do not articulate with the ideals of a heavenly people who in respect to the earth are "strangers and pilgrims" and who are enjoined to be looking for and loving the imminent appearing of Christ, the problem is easily solved by the one whose system of interpretation is proved rather than distressed by such distinctions. A plan of interpretation -- which, in defense of an ideal unity of the Bible, contends for a single divine purpose, ignores drastic contradictions, and is sustained only by occasional or accidental similarities -- is doomed to confusion when confronted with the many problems which such a system imposes on the text of Scripture, which problems are recognized by the dispensationalist only as he observes them in the system which creates them.

All Scripture is "profitable for doctrine, for reproof, for correction, for instruction in righteousness" (2 Tim. 3:16), but all Scripture is not of primary application to a particular person or class of persons which the Bible designates as such. All Scripture is not of the angels, nor is it of the Gentiles. In like manner, all Scripture is not addressed to the Jew, nor is it all addressed to the Christian. These are obvious truths and the dispensationalist's plan of interpretation is none other than an attempt to be consistent in following these distinctions in the primary application of Scripture as far as, and no further than, the Bible carries them. However, all Scripture is profitable, that is, it has its moral, spiritual, or secondary application.

To illustrate this: Much valuable truth may be gained from the great body of Scripture bearing on the Jewish Sabbath, but if that body of Scripture has a primary application to the Church, then the Church has no Biblical ground for the observance of the first day of the week (which she certainly has) and she could offer no excuse for her disobedience, and her individual members, like all Sabbath-breakers, should be stoned to death (Num. 15:32-36). In like manner, if all Scripture is of primary application to believers of this age then they are in danger of hell fire (Matt. 5:29-30), of unspeakable plagues, diseases, and sicknesses, and by reason of these to become few in number (Deut. 28:58-62), and to have the blood of lost souls required at their hands (Ezek. 3:17-18).

Moral and spiritual lessons are to be drawn from God's dealing with Israelites, quite apart from the necessity being imposed upon Christians to comply with all that a primary application of the Scriptures specifically addressed to Israel would demand. Of the believer of this age it is said that "he ... shall not come into condemnation" (John 5:24), and "there is therefore now no condemnation to them that are in Christ Jesus" (Rom. 8:1, A.R.V.). These latter promises are disannulled by diametrically opposite declarations if all Scripture applies primarily to the Christian. Arminianism is the legitimate expression of this confusion and the would-be Calvinist who ignores the plain distinction of the Bible has no defense against Arminian claims.

III. A Divinely Appointed Service
Service for God is an essential of any true religion. In the case of Judaism, service consisted in the maintenance of the tabernacle and temple ritual, and all tithes and offerings went to the support of the priesthood and their ministry. In the case of Christianity, service faces outward with its commission to preach the gospel to every creature and includes the edification of the saints.

IV. A Righteous Ground for Forgiveness and Cleansing
Any religious economy which is to continue must provide a ground upon which God is righteously free to forgive and restore those who fail. Being possessed -- as all are -- of a fallen nature, there is no possibility of anyone continuing in right relation to God who is not ever and always being renewed and restored by the gracious power of God. In the case of Judaism, God forgave sin and renewed His fellowship with them on the ground of His own certainty that a sufficient sacrifice would be made in due time by His Lamb. In the case of the Christian, God is said to be propitious concerning "our sins" (1 John 2:2), and this because of the fact that His Son has already borne the penalty (1 Cor. 15:3), and because of the fact that Christ as Advocate now appears for us when we sin (1 John 2:1). No more comforting truth can come to the Christian's heart than the assurance that God is now propitious concerning "our sins."

V. A Revelation of the Human Responsibility for Securing
Divine Forgiveness and Cleansing

This aspect of this theme offers opportunity for several
misunderstandings. In a general way, it will be recognized
by all that the requirement on the human side was, in the
Old Testament, the offering of an animal sacrifice, while in
the New Testament, following the death of Christ ·· which
event terminated all sacrifices ·· divine forgiveness for the
believer is conditioned on confession of sin, which
confession is the outward expression of an inward
repentance. All this is natural and reasonable. However,
certain complications arise when these obvious facts are
considered in their relation to other phases of truth.

It is important to observe that in the Old Testament
ages no provisions were made, so far as Scripture records,
for Gentile needs. We recognize that Abel, Noah, Job, and
Melchizedek sacrificed offerings for sin, yet no form of
doctrine is disclosed regarding these offerings. On the other
hand, the Jews, being a covenant people, were, when
injured by sin, given the sacrifices as a basis for divine
forgiveness and as a way back into those blessings and
relationships belonging to their covenants. It must be
observed that the sacrifices never constituted a ground for
the entrance into the covenants, which ground was already
secured by their physical birth, nor was any sacrifice the
ground of personal salvation. On the contrary, the
sacrifices for Israel served to provide a ground for
forgiveness and restoration of covenant people.

The parallel in Christianity is the provision through
the death of Christ whereby the Christian may be forgiven
and cleansed. Judaism required an animal sacrifice;

Christianity looks back to the sacrifice already wrought. The only parallel in Judaism of the present salvation of an unregenerate person is the fact that the Jew was physically born into his covenant relations. The personal salvation of a Jew in the old order is a theme which is yet to be considered.

VI. An Effective Basis for Worship and Prayer
Under this heading it is to be observed that the basis of an appeal on which the Old Testament saints prayed was that of their covenants. A study of the recorded prayers will disclose the fact that they pleaded with Jehovah to observe and do what He had promised He would do. The ground of prayer in the New Testament after the death, resurrection, and ascension of Christ, and the descent of the Spirit, is such that the new approach to God is in the name of Christ. Being in Christ, the believer's prayer arises to the Father as though it were the voice of Christ, and it is granted for Christ's sake. That this is new is indicated by the word of Christ when He said, "Hitherto have ye asked nothing in my name" (John 16:24). By this statement all previous forms and appeals are set aside and the new appeal is established which is as immeasurable as infinity itself. We read, "Whatsoever ye shall ask the Father in my name, he will give it you" (John 16:23).

VII. A Future Hope
Judaism has its eschatology reaching on into eternity with covenants and promises which are everlasting. On the other hand, Christianity has its eschatology which is different at every point. Some of these contrasts are:

1. The future of this life.

In the case of Israel, the thing to be desired was long life "upon the land which the Lord thy God giveth thee," whereas the Christian's hope is the prospect of the imminent coming of Christ to take away His Church from the earth. This he is taught to wait for, and he is told that he should love Christ's appearing. He has no land, nor has he any promise of earthly things beyond his personal need. In those Scriptures which warn Israel of the future coming of her Messiah, that nation is told that they should watch for His coming since that coming will be unexpected (Matt. 24:36-51; 25:13). Over against this and for the same reason, the Christian is told to wait for his Lord from heaven (1 Thess. 1:9-10).

2. The intermediate state.

One passage reporting the words of Christ is about all that Judaism reveals on the intermediate state. This is found in Luke 16:19-31. The rich man is in torment, while the beggar is in "Abraham's bosom." The latter is a strongly Jewish conception and in contrast to the revelation that when the Christian departs this life he goes to be "with Christ; which is far better" (Phil. 1:23; cf. 2 Cor. 5:8).

3. Resurrection.

Judaism contemplated a resurrection for Israel. In Daniel 12:1-3 we read that, following the great tribulation, Daniel's people will be raised from the dead (cf. Ezek. 37:1-14). Some are to be raised to everlasting life before they enter the kingdom (cf. Ezek. 37:14) and some to everlasting contempt. Rewards are also promised, for those "that be wise shall shine as the brightness of the firmament; and they that turn many to righteousness as the stars for ever and ever."

That this refers to Daniel's people is clearly indicated in the context. Martha, voicing the Jewish hope, declared that her brother would be raised again in the resurrection at the last day (John 11:24). And in Hebrews 6:1-2, where Judaism's features are named, the resurrection of the dead is included. The doctrine of resurrection for the Christian is in two parts: (a) He has already been raised and seated (Eph. 2:6), and, having partaken of the resurrection life of Christ and being positionally in the value of all Christ has done, is said to be already raised from the dead (Col. 3:1-3), and (b) should he die, the believer's body is yet to be raised, and this at the coming of Christ for His own (1 Cor. 15:23; 1 Thess. 4:16-17). The believers will also be rewarded for faithfulness in service.

4. Eternal life.

To a large degree, eschatology is the consummation of soteriology and of necessity reflects the scope and ultimate purpose of the soteriology to which it is related. To such a degree as the soteriology of Judaism and the soteriology of Christianity differ, to the same degree do their eschatologies differ. The problems which beset the soteriology of Judaism are largely due to confusion which arises when the elements which are peculiar to the soteriology of Christianity are imposed upon Judaism. The Old Testament saints were in right and acceptable relation to God, but it could not be said that they were in the new headship of the resurrected Christ, nor that their lives were "hid with Christ in God" (Col. 3:1-3).

The Apostle writes: "But before faith came, we were kept under the law, shut up unto the faith which should afterwards be revealed" (Gal. 3:23). As for the estate of the Jew in the old dispensation it may be observed: (a) They were born into covenant relations with God wherein there were no limitations imposed upon their faith in Him or upon their fellowship with Him. This fact was itself a demonstration of superabounding grace, (b) In case of failure to meet the moral and spiritual obligations resting upon them because of their covenant position, the sacrifices were provided as a righteous basis of restoration to their covenant privileges, which fact is another demonstration of immeasurable grace, (c) The individual Jew might so fail in his conduct and so neglect the sacrifices as, in the end, to be disowned of God and cast out (Gen. 17:14; Deut. 28:58-61; Ezek. 3:18; Matt. 10:32-33; 24:50-51; 25:11-12, 29-30). (d) The national salvation and forgiveness of Israel is yet a future expectation and is promised to occur when the Deliverer comes out of Sion (Rom. 11:26-27).

Who can fail to recognize the eternal grace of God revealed in Isaiah 60:1-62:12 toward Israel in all ages to come? The doctrine of eternal life as related to Israel is thought by some to present insuperable difficulties. To Israel, as is demonstrated in this thesis, eternal life was a future expectation and related to those requirements which are peculiar to Judaism. If any clarity is to be gained on the difference between Israel's privileges under the Mosaic system and the present privileges of the Church, distinction must be made between the law as a rule of life which none were able to keep perfectly, and the law as a system which not only set forth the high and holy demands upon personal conduct, but also provided complete divine forgiveness through the sacrifices. The final standing of any Jew before God was not based on law observance alone, but contemplated that Jew in the light of the sacrifices he had presented in his own behalf.

All consideration of the doctrine of eternal life, whether of one age or another, must distinguish between mere endless existence and the impartation of that life from God which is as eternal in every aspect of it as is the Author Himself. No human being can ever cease to exist; even death, which appears to terminate life, in due time will be dismissed forever (1 Cor. 15:26; Rev. 21:4). Quite apart from the indisputable fact of the endless character of human existence, is God's gracious bestowment of eternal life, which eternal life is a vital part of the eschatology of Judaism as it is a vital part of the soteriology of Christianity.

A very clear and comprehensive body of Scripture bears on eternal life as related to Judaism. However, it is there contemplated as a future inheritance. The doctrine as related to Judaism is found in well-identified passages: (a) Isaiah 55:3 (cf. Deut. 30:6), in which context the prophet is calling on a covenant people to enter fully into the blessings which Jehovah's covenants secure. In the midst of these is this promise that "your soul shall live." (b) Daniel 12:2, where the context, as seen above, relates to the resurrection of those who are of Judaism, some of these are to be raised to "everlasting life," and some to "everlasting contempt." The "life" is no more their possession in this

present existence than is the "contempt." (c) Matthew 7:13-
14, which passage is found in that portion of Scripture that
defines the terms of admission into, and conditions life in,
the earthly Messianic kingdom; which kingdom occupies a
high place in the eschatology of Judaism. The passage
imposes the most drastic human effort as essential if one
would enter the narrow way that leads to life.

The life is at the end of the path and its price is well
defined by the word *agonizomai* (better translated agonize)
as used by Luke (13:24) when this saying of Christ's is
reported by him. (d) Luke 10:25-29, in which passage the
lawyer asks how he may inherit eternal life and is told by
Christ in the most absolute terms that eternal life for him
is gained by the keeping of that contained in the Mosaic
Law -- "this do, and thou shalt live." (e) Luke 18:18-27,
where it is likewise reported that a young ruler made the
same inquiry, namely, "What shall I do to inherit eternal
life?" and to this sincere man our Lord quoted the Mosaic
commandments; but when the young man declared that
these things had been kept by him from his youth, Christ
did not chide him for falsehood but took him on to the
ground of complete surrender of all he was and all he had
as the way into that state which Christ termed perfect
(Matt. 19:21). (f) Matthew 18:8-9, which passage presents
the alternative of entering life -- a future experience --
maimed or halt, or entering "everlasting fire" or "hell fire."

That a Christian, already possessing eternal life and
perfected as he is in Christ, could not enter heaven maimed
or halt when his body is to be like Christ's glorious body,
nor into hell fire after Christ has said that he shall not
come into judgment and that he shall never perish, is

obvious indeed. Over against this extended body of
Scripture bearing on that particularized, future form of
eternal life which, being a feature of Judaism, is related to
the earthly kingdom, is another body of Scripture far more
extensive which declares that eternal life for the Christian
is an impartation from God and is the gift of God (John
10:28; Rom. 6:23); is a present possession (John 3:36; 5:24;
6:54; 20:31; 1 John 5:11-13); and is none other than Christ
indwelling (Col. 1:27) and the imparted divine nature (2
Pet. 1:4). The receiving of eternal life will be for Israelites,
as it is in the case of Christians, a feature of salvation
itself; and salvation for Israel is, in Romans 11:26-32,
declared to be after the present age-purpose of the fullness
of the Gentiles which is now accompanied by Israel's
blindness (verse 25), and at the time when "there shall
come out of Sion the Deliverer," who shall "turn away
ungodliness from Jacob." "This," Jehovah says, "is my
covenant unto them, when I shall take away their sins."
Isaiah anticipates the same great moment of Israel's
salvation when he predicts that a nation shall be born "at
once." The Hebrew words "pa'am 'ehath" from which the
words at once are translated mean, as a time
measurement, a stroke, or the beat of a foot. On the other
hand, the Christian is saved when he believes and that
salvation is related only to the first advent of Christ.

5. The Covenanted Davidic Kingdom.
This, the most extensive and important feature of the
eschatology of Judaism, occupies so large a place in the
discussion which this whole thesis presents, it need be no
more than mentioned here. That form of interpretation

which rides on occasional similarities and passes over vital differences is displayed by those who argue that the kingdom of heaven, as referred to in Matthew, must be the same as the kingdom of God since some parables regarding the kingdom of heaven are reported in Mark and Luke under the designation the kingdom of God. No attempt is made by these expositors to explain why the term kingdom of heaven is used by Matthew only, nor do they seem to recognize the fact that the real difference between that which these designations represent is to be discovered in connection with the instances where they are not and cannot be used interchangeably rather than in the instances where they are interchangeable.

Certain features are common to both the kingdom of heaven and the kingdom of God, and in such instances the interchange of the terms is justified. Closer attention will reveal that the kingdom of heaven is always earthly while the kingdom of God is as wide as the universe and includes as much of earthly things as are germane to it. Likewise, the kingdom of heaven is entered by a righteousness exceeding the righteousness of the scribes and Pharisees (Matt. 5:20), while the kingdom of God is entered by a new birth (John 3:1-16). So, again, the kingdom of heaven answers the hope of Israel and the Gentiles, while the kingdom of God answers the eternal and all-inclusive purpose of God. To be more explicit: Matthew 5:20 declares the condition upon which a Jew might hope to enter the kingdom of heaven. Matthew 8:12; 24:50-51; 25:28-30 indicate that children of the kingdom of heaven are to be cast out. Neither of these truths could apply to the kingdom of God. Again, the parables of the wheat and the tares,

Matthew 13:24-30, 36-43, and the parable of the good and bad fish, Matthew 13:47-50, are spoken only of the kingdom of heaven. However, the parable of the leaven is predicated of both spheres of divine rule; leaven, representing evil doctrine rather than evil persons, may corrupt, as it does, the truth relative to both kingdoms. Such contrasts might be cited to great lengths, but the important objective has been gained if it has been made clear that there is an eschatology of Judaism and an eschatology of Christianity and each, though wholly different in details, reaches on into eternity. One of the great burdens of predictive prophecy is the anticipation of the glories of Israel in a transformed earth under the reign of David's Son, the Lord Jesus Christ, the Son of God. There is likewise much prediction which anticipates the glories of the redeemed in heaven.

No division of theology is more beset with problems than soteriology. The plan of salvation itself is the solution of the question of how Jehovah might remain just and at the same time justify a sinner who does no more than to believe in Jesus (Rom. 3:26). The difficulties are no less in the soteriology of Judaism than in the soteriology of Christianity. The ultimate holy estate of each group is such that God will be equally free to tabernacle with them both. In 2 Peter 3:13 it is stated with reference to the new heaven and the new earth that in them alike righteousness will dwell; the implication being that the new earth will be inhabited. Israel's fundamental covenants are both earthly and eternal and their national entity is forever identified with the earth (Isa. 66:22).

Revelation 21:3-4 is a description of the new earth. This is evident from the earthly designation "men" and from the fact that the "former things," said to have "passed away," are only earthly in character. It is said that God will tabernacle among men. The saints of the former dispensations were sanctified, that is, they were set apart unto God. Their very birth into the covenant rights was advantageous to a surpassing degree. They were granted the experience of relief from the condemnation of their sins through the sacrifices, and they were on a ground of fellowship with God and temporal blessings when in right relation to Him. Faith toward God was a most vital part of their daily life and by it some wrought great accomplishments (Heb. 11:4-38); but it must not be overlooked that "these all, having obtained a good report through faith, received not the promise: God having provided some better thing for us, that they without us should not be made perfect" (vss. 39-40). This passage not only declares the delay in the execution of Israel's promises, but distinguishes between the blessings covenanted to Israel and the "better things" which belong to "us."

Again, we read concerning the same Jewish saints: "These all died in faith, not having received the promises, but having seen them afar off, and were persuaded of them, and embraced them, and confessed that they were strangers and pilgrims on the earth" (Heb. 11:13). Thus it is clear that of the blessings which Judaism provided, some temporal and spiritual experiences were immediately secured through adjustment to the Mosaic system; but the larger features of the taking away of sin, the receiving of eternal life, and the kingdom glories were reserved for the return of their King.

Chapter IV
Dispensationalism in the
Light of Divine Grace

Chapter IV
Dispensationalism in the
Light of Divine Grace

When contemplating more specifically the precise character of each divine economy, it is essential that the nature, extent, and scope of God's grace shall be carefully estimated. At least three aspects of the doctrine of grace are involved, namely:

I. The Divine Freedom to Act in Behalf of Sinful Men
Unlike His wisdom, power, and glory, which could be manifested in creation, the grace of God could be manifested only as there were fallen beings toward whom He could be gracious. It is difficult to believe that the exercise of this essential part of His nature would be suppressed forever, or that, when it is expressed, it would not be on a plane as perfect and as worthy of Him as are all His works. In verses 4 and 5 of the context of Ephesians 2:1-10, which context is the central passage of the Bible on divine grace, three closely related words appear ·· mercy, love, and grace.

A distinction is here indicated: Love is the affection or compassion of God for sinners; mercy is that in Him which devised and provided a redemption through the death of His Son; while grace, in its outworking, is that which God is free to do on the ground of that death. God might love sinners with an unutterable compassion and yet, because of the demands of outraged justice and holiness, be precluded from rescuing them from their righteous doom. The essential revelation contained in the gospel of our salvation is this fact that God is now free within Himself to act in grace toward sinners through the death of Christ for them. Since no other freedom to act in behalf of sinners has been secured, it is to be concluded that all God has ever done or will do for sinful men is wrought on the sole basis of Christ's death. Even though Christ has died and God is thus free to act in grace, the question of whether He does little or much for men will be determined only according to His sovereign purpose. This freedom He will always exercise as He has exercised it in past ages.

II. The Divine Purpose in this Age: A Complete Demonstration of Grace

As stated above, whatever God has done in behalf of man in any age, being based on the death of Christ, is a manifestation of grace; but the present, unforeseen age is unique in this that its divine purpose is, to a distinguishing degree, the supreme demonstration of God's grace. Had this distinction been observed, a number of misunderstandings regarding dispensational truth would have been obviated. Because it is believed that this age is peculiarly one of divine favor does not militate against the belief that God's grace is abundantly exercised in all other ages. Proofs that this is an age in which God is manifesting

His grace are many indeed. Two of these will suffice: (1) In Matthew 13:1-50 the present age is in view under seven parables. They treat of a divine economy when "the field is the world," which breadth of view did not obtain from Abraham to Christ. Three elements are to be distinguished in these parables, namely, (a) that which is good, designated as "wheat," "good seed," the "pearl of great price," and the "good fish"; (b) that which is evil, designated as "tares," evil "birds," "leaven," and "bad fish"; and (c) the "treasure" hid in the field, which so evidently refers to Israel, as the "pearl of great price" so evidently refers to the Church.

Thus three elements appear in this description of the present age, namely, that which is good, or the heavenly people; that which is evil, or the unregenerate masses; and the earthly people, Israel. Two New Testament passages add much to this revelation. In 2 Thessalonians 2:7 it is disclosed that the Restrainer, who many expositors agree is the Holy Spirit, goes on restraining until He is taken out of the way. This important passage records the fact that the Spirit, who is ever omnipresent but specifically resident in the world in this age, will leave the world. However, according to John 14:16-17, the Church in which He now dwells cannot be separated from Him. Thus it is demonstrated that the age-purpose is not the cessation of evil, but rather the completion of the Church. This truth is even more clearly presented in Romans 11:25 where Israel's present blindness (Isa. 6:9-10; Matt. 13:14-15; John 12:40; 2 Cor. 3:14-15) is declared to continue until the "fulness of the Gentiles be come in." "The fulness of the

Gentiles" is a designation which is explained in Ephesians 1:22-23 as "the church, which is his body."

Thus we observe that of the three elements which characterize this age, neither Israel's program, nor a victory over evil is the purpose of this age, but that each of these is waiting until the Church is called out. (2) In Ephesians 2:4-10 it is directly stated that salvation, as now provided through Christ, is secured by faith alone, with the purpose in view that in the ages to come God may by means of it "shew the exceeding riches of his grace." Of three motives assigned to God for His present saving grace (cf. Eph. 2:7; John 3:16), the fact that by the present exercise of saving grace He will make a demonstration to all intelligences of the "exceeding riches" of His grace, is that which surpasses all else in the measure in which God is greater than man. Of no other age -- those recorded in history or those anticipated in prophecy -- could it be said that its primary divine purpose is the making by God of a specific demonstration, all satisfying to Himself, of His grace. Likewise, in no other age could it be said that those who are saved are "accepted in the beloved"; yet this very acceptance, which is divine favor drawn out to infinity, is said to be "to the praise of the glory of his grace" (Eph. 1:6).

It may be concluded that the present primary age-purpose of God is the demonstration of His grace, which belief in no way precludes one from recognizing the gracious acts of God in all other ages. What worthy Bible expositor has ever contended for aught else than this concerning the grace of God?

III. God's Grace in Covenant Form

Whatever God declares He will do is always a binding covenant. If He in no way relates His proposed action to human responsibility, the covenant is properly termed unconditional. If He relates it to human responsibility or makes it to depend on cooperation on the part of any other being, the covenant is properly termed conditional. It may be contended that there is no unconditional, or conditional, covenant which God has made; but it must be admitted that, contemplating these propositions even hypothetically, they do represent principles which can in no way combine. A covenant which is unconditional cannot be conditional and a conditional covenant cannot be unconditional. While all the covenants God has made with men cannot be treated here, it is essential that these fundamental elements in the divine economy shall be emphasized.

1. An unconditional covenant.

Because of the fact that human obedience is indirectly related to some aspects of the unconditional divine covenants, confusion seems to exist in the minds of certain writers. It is identically the same confusion which hinders many from recognizing the present marvels of salvation by grace and prompts men to get the "cart" of human works before the "horse" of faith, or, in some instances, the horse is in the cart or even under the cart as fancy dictates.

As before stated, whatever God does for sinful man on any terms whatsoever, being made possible through the death of Christ, is, to that extent, an act of divine grace; for whatever God does on the ground of Christ's death is gracious in character, and all will agree that a divine covenant which is void of all human elements is more gracious in character than one which is otherwise. These distinctions apply only to the divine side of any covenant. On the human side ·· a theme yet to be considered ·· there is no exercise of grace in any case; but the human requirements which the divine covenant imposes may be either absolutely lacking or so drastically imposed as to determine the destiny of the individual. When any person becomes the beneficiary of God's unconditional, unalterable promise apart from any consideration of human merit, his obligation for righteous conduct becomes that of adorning, or walking worthy, of the position into which the covenant has brought him.

If God has made a covenant declaring what He will do provided man does his part, it is conditional and the human element is not one of walking worthy of what God's sovereign grace provides, but rather one of being worthy to the end that the promise may be executed at all. When the covenant is unconditional, God is limited in what He will do only by the knowledge-surpassing bounty of His infinite grace. When the covenant is conditional, God is restricted by what man is able or willing to do. As an efficacious appeal, the obligation to walk worthy, though in no way conditioning the sovereign purpose, secures more normal and spiritual response than all the meritorious systems combined. The human heart is far more responsive to the proposition couched in the words "I have blessed you, now be good," than it is to the proposition couched in the words "Be good, and I will bless you." The element of human conduct thus appears in each form of the divine covenant but in such a manner that one is rendered unconditional and the other conditional.

One further distinction is essential before turning to an evaluation of three unconditional covenants, namely, God's unconditional and sovereign dealing with Israel is to the end that they are an elect nation. Concerning the nation as an entity, it is said, "For the gifts and callings of God are without repentance" (Rom. 11:29). And this context cannot be of any other than national Israel. But this national election does not extend to every Israelite. That it does not, the Apostle proves in Romans 9:1-24. On the contrary, the individual Israelite, when under the Mosaic Law, was, in the matter of his personal blessing, under a secondary, meritorious covenant with gracious provisions in the animal sacrifices for the covering and cure of his sins and failures.

In sharp distinction to this, the Church is, in respect to her corporate whole, an elect people also (Rom. 8:33), but her election and sovereign security is extended to every individual in that body (John 5:24; 6:37; 10:28; Rom. 8:1, A.R.V.). While Israel anticipated much of her blessings, the Church now possesses "every spiritual blessing ... in Christ" (Eph. 1:3, A.R.V.; Col. 2:10). Distinction should also be made between the blessings and privileges within the covenants and the terms of admission into the covenants. In the case of the Israelite, entrance into the covenants was by physical birth; while in the case of the Christian it is by spiritual birth. The gospel terms upon which a Christian has entered into a grace relationship with God are no more a part of the believer's positions than the physical birth of an Israelite was a part of the covenants under which he lived. The unconditional covenants to be considered are:

a. The Abrahamic Covenant.
Though in part it was repeated to Isaac and Jacob, the full detail of the Abrahamic Covenant as given to Abraham is found in five passages of Scripture: Genesis 12:1-3; 12:7; 13:14-17; 15:5-21; 17:1-8. This covenant provides for a blessing to extend to all the families of the earth; it provides for one great nation -- Abraham's seed after the flesh; it deeds a vast territory to that nation as an everlasting possession; and assures a personal blessing to Abraham himself. The feature of this covenant which concerns the land is amplified by the terms found in the Palestinian Covenant (Deut. 28:63-68; 30:1-10) and, while the everlasting possession of the land is declared, other Scriptures reveal that there were to be three dispossessions of the land and three restorations.

It is also evident that the nation to whom this land is deeded is now, as a divine chastisement, suffering the third and last dispossession of the land; but will, in the faithfulness of Jehovah, be returned to her land, never again to be removed from it. It is recognized that great numbers of the Israelites have gone back into the land in unbelief within recent years, and by so much prophecy is fulfilled. The Abrahamic Covenant, aside from that portion which is addressed to Abraham personally, could be executed only as Jehovah in sovereign power commands the destiny of all future generations of the human family. Thus, since any human terms which might have been imposed could apply only to individual men and to their own generation, the covenant is, of necessity, unconditional; and the statement of it incorporates not one human condition, but rests altogether on the oft-repeated sovereign "I will" of Jehovah. Added to all this, the ratification of the covenant as described in Genesis 15:5-21 is most significant. In response to Abraham's appeal for a ratification, Jehovah instructs Abraham in the preparation of the carcasses which, when half was put over against half, formed a passageway between, through which the covenanting parties passed; but Abraham is depressed into a very deep sleep while Jehovah, in the appearance of a burning lamp, passes through alone. The reason for this is that Abraham covenanted nothing; it is the ratification only of Jehovah's sovereign oath (Gen. 26:3).

Recent extensive arguments have been advanced in an attempt to prove that since the human element appears in a covenant, there is no such thing as an unconditional covenant. The ineffectiveness of these arguments lies in the failure of the writer to distinguish between that form of conduct which belongs to one already secure in all that the covenant provides, and, on the other hand, the direct conditioning of Jehovah's faithfulness upon human rectitude. The Abrahamic Covenant is sealed by the rite of circumcision, which seal can be no more than the individual's personal recognition of what Jehovah has promised. Failure thus to recognize Jehovah's covenant imposed a penalty on the individual, but did not alter Jehovah's covenant reaching out to the nation and to all families of the earth. The charge which Jehovah makes against the offender is not that he hath broken our covenant, but, rather, "he hath broken my covenant" (Gen. 17:14).

It has also been asserted that the Abrahamic Covenant was made conditional upon Abraham's faithfulness. Only two passages might thus be misconstrued. Genesis 17:9-14 does not present a condition restricting Jehovah's "I will" to Abraham's conduct. It rather instructs Abraham in the manner of life which becomes one for whom Jehovah undertakes so much. In like manner, Genesis 26:5 is not addressed to Abraham, but is rather Jehovah's declaration to Isaac extending to him the sovereign, unconditional covenant made to his father Abraham. Isaac is admonished to live a faithful life under the covenant "because" of the example of his father. In this connection, the exact reading of Genesis 18:19 is significant.

In this context Jehovah says: "For I have known him [as a factor in my gracious purpose], to the end [or result] that he [Abraham] may command his children and his household after him, that they may keep the way of Jehovah, to do righteousness and justice; to the end that Jehovah may bring upon Abraham [in personal blessing] that which he hath spoken of him" (A.R.V.). In the contemplation of these important issues, two outstanding, qualifying facts should be observed: (1) No human element appears in any feature of the Abrahamic Covenant as it is announced by Jehovah, and (2) that both Abraham's position in Jehovah's covenant to him and Abraham's imputed righteousness (Gen. 15:6) are secured to him apart from meritorious works. Romans 4:1-22 declares that Abraham's blessings both concerning imputed righteousness and his position as "heir of the world" (vs. 13) were wholly secured before he was circumcised (vs. 10). Thus, also, it is asserted that, in contrast to the "works principle" which the Mosaic system introduces, Jehovah gave Abraham the inheritance contained in the Abrahamic Covenant by "promise," namely, what He alone did promise by an oath to do (Gal. 3:13-18). All of this bears vitally on the present offers of salvation by grace which are not by works (Eph. 2:8-9), but by promise (Gal. 3:22; cf. Rom. 4:23-25; Gal. 3:9).

Thus the Apostle Paul declares that to intrude the element of human works into the Abrahamic Covenant, or as a ground of that righteousness which was imputed to Abraham, is to intrude works into the present plan of salvation by grace. To do this is no small error indeed, for it makes the promise of "none effect" when God has made it "sure" (Rom. 4:13-16). In the light of all these revelations, what subtle Arminianism infests the doctrine of those who claim that Jehovah made His covenant with Abraham on the ground of the fact that Abraham was one who "obeyed my voice, and kept my charge, my commandments, my statutes, and my laws" (Gen. 26:5). The Abrahamic Covenant is unconditional, else, by such logic as only the Apostle could use, a passage like Ephesians 2:7-10 becomes null and void.

b. The Davidic Covenant.
2 Samuel 7:16 with its context records the covenant Jehovah made with David. David's own interpretation of it is written in 2 Samuel 7:18-29 and in Psalm 89:20-37. This covenant, without imposing the slightest obligation upon

David, does bind Jehovah with an oath (Acts 2:30) to the perpetuity of the Davidic house, the Davidic throne, and the Davidic kingdom. Again, Jehovah reserves the right to chasten the sons of David, but with the express declaration that the covenant cannot be abrogated (2 Sam. 7:13-15; Ps. 89:30-37).

This covenant is unconditional, even into eternity to come. It declares what Jehovah in grace will do for David and all who share in the Davidic blessings. The covenant is of an earthly throne related to a people whose expectation is earthly. There is no evidence that David foresaw an earthly throne merging into a spiritual reign, yet David was given a perfect understanding concerning the divine purpose which the covenant designated. Nor is this kingdom and throne established in heaven. It is established on the earth when the Son of David returns to the earth (Matt. 25:31-32; cf. 19:28; Acts 15:16-17; Luke 1:31-33; Matt. 2:2). In the light of the unqualified statements of the Scriptures, is it not pertinent to inquire whether, had Jehovah intended to establish a Davidic throne and kingdom on earth with David's Son as the eternal occupant of that throne, He could have employed language with any more clearness and precise meaning than He has employed to set forth the covenant made with David?

c. The Gospel of Divine Grace.

Many worthy expositors combine the present offers of salvation, as being the outworking of the New Covenant made in Christ's blood (Matt. 26:28), with the long-predicted New Covenant yet to be made with Israel (Jer.

31:31-40; Heb. 8:8-13; 10:16-17), and on the ground that the term new covenant is used of both and because it is believed that the term is broad enough to include all that God accomplishes directly through the blood of Christ. However, there are such important differences between that which God is doing for the heavenly people over against that which He will yet do for Israel and the Gentiles on the earth in the kingdom age, that the two, even though they might be parts of one grand whole, should be considered separately.

As cited above, the absolute, unconditional character of the Abrahamic Covenant and the fact that all that Abraham received was by promise, concerning which Abraham did no more than to believe, is declared by the Apostle to be the norm or pattern of the saving grace of God for the believer of this age (Rom. 4:1-25; note vss. 23-25; Gal. 3:13-29).

Dr. Allis (Evangelical Quarterly, Edinburgh, Vol. VIII, No. 1, p. 29) criticizes the late Dr. Scofield for distinguishing at least four uses of the word gospel. Since Dr. Allis centers this criticism upon the distinction between the gospel of the kingdom and the gospel of the grace of God and suggests that to recognize a difference between them is "unfortunate" and "dangerous," attention is called to four out of many important differences between them: (a) The gospel of the kingdom as preached by Christ, by John the Baptist, and by the Apostles is declared and amplified in an extensive body of Scripture (cf. Matt. 3:1-12; 4:17; 10:5-42; Luke 3:7-14). Its distinctive "good news" is the announcement of the presence of the long-expected Messiah and His predicted blessings for Israel. Over against this, the gospel of the grace of God is even more extensive and announces a plan of perfect salvation for Jew and Gentile alike. (b) The kingdom gospel, since it concerns Israel's national hope, was properly restricted to them. The heralds of this gospel went not to Gentile nor Samaritan, but only to the lost sheep of the house of Israel (Matt. 10:5-7; 15:24, 26); whereas the gospel of the grace of God is to be preached to all nations and to the uttermost part of the earth, (c) The one and only requirement on the human side which the kingdom gospel imposes is repentance, while the only requirement in the gospel of the grace of God is faith or believing.

A covenant people return to the blessing of their covenants, when these have been lost through sin, by repentance and its outward expression -- confession (Ps. 32:5; Matt. 4:17; 1 John 1:9). On the other hand, the requirement on the human side for present salvation is belief in Christ as Savior, which belief includes all the repentance (which is a change of mind) that a spiritually dead person can produce. John's Gospel, written that men may be saved through faith in Christ, and the Epistle to the Romans, which is the very structure of the plan of salvation, do not use the word repentance as a separate act in salvation, nor is anything added, nor could anything be added reasonably, to the one and only requirement -- believe. However, believing as related to the Messiah must be distinguished from believing unto salvation. Since the first preaching of the kingdom gospel called for repentance only, it is evident that it was addressed to a covenant people, and it is to be noted that Israel was the only covenant people in that day. It is also evident that this gospel call was not for the salvation even of Israel, but was for their revival and restoration, (d) Since according to Matthew 10:7-8 signs were to accompany the kingdom preaching -- healing, cleansing of the lepers, raising of the dead, and casting out demons, and this they did (cf. Luke 10:17) -- this seal is an inseparable feature of kingdom preaching.

On the other hand, though certain miracles were wrought by the early preachers of the grace gospel, no signs were ever promised as an accompanying seal. Similarly, what place has Matthew 10:22 or 24:13 in a Calvinistic conception of salvation? The question may be asked in all kindness of Dr. Allis and all men of his school of interpretation: How many men have been led to a saving knowledge of a crucified and risen Savior by calling on them to repent for the kingdom of heaven is at hand? And has this preaching been accompanied by the designated miracles which are the seal of a kingdom ministry?

According to this norm and in exact harmony with its every feature, the Christian's salvation and safekeeping, which are in the sphere of the very perfections of Christ, are vouchsafed to him on the most absolute unconditional promises (cf. John 5:24; 6:37; 10:27-30; Rom. 3:21--5:11; 8:1, 28-39; Eph. 1:3-6; Col. 2:10). Faith is itself the opposite of works, since its essential element is confidence in what Christ had done and can do; but, as has been seen, the condition of entrance into a relationship is no part of the relationship itself. The very fact that present salvation is declared to be to the end that a full demonstration of the exceeding riches of divine grace may be wrought out, necessitates its being altogether a work of God and, therefore, unconditional.

d. The New Covenant for Israel.

A new covenant for Israel is anticipated in Jeremiah 31:31-40; Hebrews 8:8-13; 10:16-17. This is not to supersede the Abrahamic and Davidic Covenants which continue forever, but is put over against that Mosaic Covenant which Jehovah declares that Israel "brake" (Jer. 31:32) and in which they "continued not" (Heb. 8:9). The contrast is emphatic, and in no respect more so than in the fact that the Mosaic Covenant was subject to human conditions concerning which Israel failed, while the New Covenant for that people is declared in the most explicit terms to be unconditional.

We read: "After those days, saith the Lord, I will put my law in their inward parts, and write it in their hearts; and will be their God, and they shall be my people. And they shall teach no more every man his neighbour, and every man his brother, saying, Know the Lord: for they shall all know me, from the least of them unto the greatest of them, saith the Lord: for I will forgive their iniquity, and I will remember their sin no more" (Jer. 31:33-34). According to Deuteronomy 30:1-10, the execution of all that this covenant promises is related to the return of Christ; in Romans 11:26-27 to the Deliverer who comes "out of Sion"; and in Jeremiah it is related to the eternal existence of the nation Israel (31:35-37). No human condition can be forced into this great declaration of Jehovah's concerning what He will yet do for Israel, nor can it be demonstrated that such promises have ever been fulfilled for Israel, nor that they even remotely apply to the Church.

When a parallel is drawn between the New Covenant now in force for the Church (Matt. 26:28) and the New Covenant yet to be made for Israel (Jer. 31:31-34), it is found that all that is promised Israel is now vouchsafed to the Church and that the range of blessing for the Church far exceeds the restricted provisions for Israel, (a) Jehovah's law will be written on the heart of the Jew, but God by His indwelling Spirit is now working in the believer both to will and to do of His good pleasure (Phil. 2:13; cf. Rom. 8:4). (b) Jehovah will be Israel's God and they will be His people, but the Christian is now in Christ and his life is now "hid with Christ in God" (Col. 3:3). (c) All Israel shall know the Lord, but the Christian is in the most vital union and communion with God as Father, (d) Israel's iniquities will be forgiven and her sins remembered no more, but for the one in Christ judicial forgiveness is secured to the extent that there is now no condemnation to those who are in Christ Jesus (Rom. 8:1), and they have been forgiven all trespasses (Col. 2:13).

The theological term the Covenant of Grace is not found in the text of the Scriptures. From the literature bearing upon it, it is to be concluded that it is believed by many that all that God does for the benefit of man from the fall of Adam to the end of time is incorporated into one "Covenant of Grace." This supposed covenant, though not identified in its beginning, course, or ending, is seldom declared to be unconditional. In considering this theological conception, it is well to observe that any covenant in which God is free to act on the ground of Christ's death has the element of grace in it, and any covenant which publishes God's sovereign declaration of what He will do for sinful men apart from their merit or demerit is specifically a grace covenant.

The term the Covenant of Grace implies that there is but one such covenant, whereas the Scriptures, as demonstrated above, present various, wholly independent, and diverse covenants which are both sovereign and gracious to the last conceivable degree. Grace on the part of the First Person, secured and made righteously possible by the Second Person, and administered by the Third Person, has been and must continue to be the attitude of the Triune God toward lost men until the divine purposes in grace are realized. If the term the Covenant of Grace refers to an agreement of the Three Persons of the Godhead between themselves concerning the part each would assume in the plan of redemption, as some contend, such an agreement is conceivable, but is not clearly revealed in the Scriptures. If, as others contend, this covenant refers to the abiding purpose of God to act toward sinners in grace, it can be classed as a covenant only in so far as a purpose of God can be considered to be a covenant. If this latter conception is accepted, it must be conceded that the working out of this one abiding purpose is expressed in various, diverse, and wholly independent ways.

2. A conditional covenant.

The phrase the Covenant of Works is another theological conception which by some is claimed to be an agreement between God and Adam concerning Adam's conduct in the Garden of Eden, and, since Adam's failure secured the ruin of the race, all are included in the condemnation. However, man still has an inherent obligation to be in character like his Creator, and in one subsequent covenant, at least, which God has made with man, the human element is such that it determines the entire course of the covenant's blessing. This latter covenant is conditional, and, though of the same nature as the covenant with Adam, is wholly separate from and independent of it.

A conditional covenant is formed when God, to any degree or in any form whatsoever, makes His blessings to depend on human faithfulness. At first thought it might seem to some that, since various major covenants, cited above, reach out in unconditional promises and provisions to Abraham's seed, both physical and spiritual, and to all the families of the earth, that there could be no sphere left in which any conditional covenant might be formed. It will be observed, however, that the Abrahamic and Davidic Covenants, which reach out to Israel and the nations for all time to come, do not, beyond certain men ·· Abraham, Isaac, Jacob, David, David's immediate sons, and David's Greater Son, Christ ·· enter into any personal or individual issues; but concern the larger entities of families, thrones, kings, and nations. This fact necessitates the recognition of a sphere wherein God deals with individuals about their personal conduct. This He did with individual Jews and this He does with individual Christians. His attitude toward a nation or corporate body is one thing, whereas His requirements of the individual within these groups is quite another thing.

Again, a distinction should be observed between the basis on which God placed individual Israelites regarding personal conduct and the basis on which He places the Christian. The national covenants with Israel do not extend to the individual; they guarantee the perpetuity of the race or nation and its final blessing. When under the Mosaic Law the individual Israelite, it will be seen, was on an unyielding meritorious basis. Over against this, the divine purposes for the whole Church as a body do extend to the individual believer and every one predestinated will be called, and every one called will be justified, and every one justified will be glorified (Rom. 8:30). God will present each one faultless before the presence of His glory to His own exceeding joy (Jude 1:24). The believer's motive for right conduct grows out of the fact that he already has an eternal heavenly calling and a destiny which sovereign grace has designed and will execute to infinite perfection. Thus, in like manner, the Mosaic Law, even if observed, never had the function of creating Israelites; it was given as a consistent rule of life to those who were Israelites by physical birth.

As has been seen, the blessings proffered to the individual Israelite under the law were in two classifications: (a) For faithful observance of the law which included the remedial value of the sacrifices, they were promised immediate prosperity and tranquility. This truth appears in almost every statement of the Mosaic Law, and nowhere more clearly than in Deuteronomy 28:1-62 where both the blessings and curses which the law imposed are set forth. (b) For faithfulness under the law they were promised a share in the future glories which Jehovah, with unconditional sovereignty, covenanted to the nation. Not every Israelite will enter the earthly kingdom (Ezek. 20:33-

44; Matt. 24:48-51; 25:1-13, 14-30). Nor will every Israelite have right to eternal life (Dan. 12:2; Matt. 7:13-14; Luke 10:25-28). Since human faithfulness of whatever degree could never be the exact compensation or exchange for the values of eternal life or for unending blessings in the kingdom, there is a very large measure of divine grace to be seen in the salvation of the elect earthly people.

What is identified as a spiritual remnant in Israel, seen in all her generations from Moses to Christ, is none other than those who through personal faithfulness claimed the immediate blessings which the law provided. Some Israelites did live on a very high plane and were in very much personal blessing. To this a multitude of Old Testament saints bear witness (Heb. 11:1-38) and none are more conspicuous in their worthy conduct than Daniel. When looking back upon his experience in Judaism, the Apostle Paul could say that he had then been, as "touching the righteousness which is in the law, blameless" (Phil. 3:6). This did not imply sinless perfection, but rather that he had always provided the requisite sacrifices. On that basis the faithful Jew lived and was accepted of God in the Mosaic system. Who, indeed, are the "ninety and nine just persons who need no repentance" cited by Christ according to Luke 15:7? And why were other covenant people classified as "publicans and sinners"?

After a new order is established through the death and resurrection of Christ, men like Nicodemus, the Apostles, and Saul of Tarsus were saved by a new birth, not because they were utter failures in Judaism, but because a new and vastly different relation to God was provided. Why should Saul who before the law was blameless need to be saved at all? Why should three thousand covenant people be saved on the Day of Pentecost? After the new gospel of grace with its offers of a perfect standing in Christ apart from human merit was established, the Apostle complains that unsaved Jews, who as he confessed had a great zeal for God, were still going about to establish their own righteousness and were not through faith coming under the perfect merit of the imputed righteousness of God (Rom. 10:3). In this connection he declares, "For Christ is the end of the law for righteousness to every one that believeth" (vs. 4).

The conclusion is that blessing under the Mosaic economy was conditioned on individual faithfulness to the law. This economy formed a secondary covenant which was meritorious in character ·· secondary in the fact that it was restricted to the problems concerning the individual's conduct and in no way compromising the primary covenants which determine the destiny of the nation. In contrast to this, the Christian, while given a rule of life which is in no way meritorious though his faithful service will win a reward or divine recognition (1 Cor. 3:12-15; 9:19-27; 2 Cor. 5:9-11), is in regard to his personal salvation ·· like the corporate whole to which he belongs ·· both secure and safe and destined to eternal glory from the moment he believes.

The Mosaic Covenant of works, which Micah perfectly epitomized was an ad interim economy: "He hath shewed thee, O man, what is good; and what doth the Lord require of thee, but to do justly, and to love mercy, and to walk humbly with thy God?" (6:8). It was preceded by a peculiar divine freedom and reign of grace by which they had reached the very heart of God (Ex. 19:4), and it came to its determined end with the death of Christ (John 1:17; Rom. 3:21; 6:14; 7:2-6; 8:3-4; 10:4; 2 Cor. 3:7-13; Gal. 3:19-25). The Word of God everywhere harmonizes with the revelation that the Mosaic economy as a rule of life came to its end with the death of Christ. However, this statement involves a long discussion with a recognition of the various uses of the word law as found in the New Testament. Space precludes the introduction of such a study as a feature of this thesis.

It is true that Jehovah had determined the law as the rule of life for the Israelites, yet it is equally true that they embraced this law and assumed their part in a conditional covenant when they said, "All the words which the Lord hath said will we do" (cf. Rom. 9:30-33); and it is significant that this people, who before had been drawn to the heart of God, found Him, after their consent to this covenant, hidden behind an unapproachable fire and surrounded by blackness and darkness (Ex. 19:8-25; cf. Heb. 12:18-24). They found themselves standing on a covenant of works, but without the requisite merit. The gracious provisions for healing and restoration which were in the sacrifices became their only hope.

If the Mosaic Covenant was not one of works and conditioned by human merit, as some have claimed, what was the "yoke of bondage" (Gal. 5:1; cf. Acts 15:10)? What covenant was "cast out" (Gal. 4:19-31)? And what is the old covenant said to have been given to them when they came out of Egypt and which they "brake" (Jer. 31:31-34; Heb. 8:7-13)? It is opposed to truth to claim that the law is no longer a means to justification. When was it ever a justifying agency? True, men became "just" men by its observance (cf. Luke 6:1-5), but that is far removed from the Christian's absolutely perfect justification apart from law works (Rom. 4:5-6; 5:1) in Christ Jesus. It is equally unwarranted to impose the meritorious Mosaic Covenant of works as a rule of life upon a people who already stand in the finished work of Christ (Gal. 2:16; Eph. 1:6). Much that is vital in the law system is restated and incorporated in the principles which instruct the believer in his manner of life under grace, but this fact does not place the Christian under law. It is probable that certain features of the law which governed the thirteen colonies under English authority were incorporated in and adapted to the legal system which afterwards became the law of the United States, but that fact would not be sufficient ground for the claim that the United States is now under the rule of England.

The rule governing the conduct of Israelites is in two principal divisions, namely, (a) that which obtained from Moses to Christ, or the Mosaic Law, and (b) that which determines entrance into and conditions life within the future kingdom on the earth. The terms of admission into the kingdom as set forth in Matthew 5:1-7:27 are, in reality, the Mosaic requirements intensified by Christ's own interpretation of them. The contrasts which He draws between the former interpretation of these laws and His own interpretation (Matt. 5:21-44) does not tend to soften anything in the interests of grace, but rather binds with greater legal demands than any unaided person in the present age could hope to achieve. Why are the plain injunctions of Matthew 5:39-42; 10:8-14 and 24:20 so universally ignored today if it is not that it is so generally recognized that these injunctions belong to conditions obtaining in another age? Will not the exalted demands of the Sermon on the Mount be more easily obeyed when earthly conditions are changed, as they will be?

The Church will be removed and Israel advanced to a position above all the nations of the earth with Jehovah's Law written in their hearts and the Spirit poured out on all flesh. Satan will be bound and in the abyss; the present world-system will have been destroyed; the bondage of corruption now resting upon creation will be lifted; and Christ as the glorified Son of David will be reigning on David's throne out from Jerusalem and over the whole earth. The effect of that reign will be that righteousness and peace shall cover the earth as waters cover the face of the deep. These conceptions are drawn from a vast body of Scripture which could have no other meaning than that which is here set forth. When these great issues which are so definitely related to Israel are applied to the heavenly people as some apply them, there are insuperable conflicts created in doctrine which lead one to inquire (and the questions will be confined, in the main, to the problems that arise from the careful consideration of but one book of the Bible):

1. As a title, what is the meaning of the designation, The Christ?
2. Why was Christ born of the Davidic line?
3. Is such a birth essential if His kingdom is spiritual?
4. Why should He be designated "THE KING OF THE JEWS"?

5. Was the ministry of John the Baptist in anticipation of a spiritual kingdom?

6. Why was the kingdom message restricted to Israel?

7. What is the "hope" of Israel?

8. Into what kingdom does any man enter by personal righteousness?

9. Are the heavenly people referred to as "the meek" who are to inherit the earth?

10. How can Matthew 5:7 be reconciled with Ephesians 2:4-5?

11. How can Christians who according to John 10:28 are safe in Christ be in danger of the hell fire mentioned in Matthew 5:22, 29-30?

12. Will a Christian, who is promised a glorious body like unto Christ's resurrection body (Phil. 3:20-21), nevertheless enter heaven "halt" and "maimed"? See Matthew 5:29-30; 18:8-9.

13. What is the doctrinal relation between Matthew 5:17 and Romans 15:8-9?

14. Can Matthew 5:20 be reconciled with Titus 3:4-7?

15. How can the difference be accounted for between Matthew 7:21-23 and John 6:29?

16. How can Matthew 10:32-33 be reconciled with Romans 8:30; 2 Timothy 1:12; or 1 John 2:1-2?

17. How can Christ appear as prosecutor in Matthew 10:32-33 and as defender in 1 John 2:1-2?

18. How can Matthew 7:1-2 be reconciled with John 5:24?

19. Why is the "golden rule" of Matthew 7:12 related to "the law and the prophets"?

20. Are Christians referred to as "children of the kingdom" in Matthew 8:12 (cf. 24:50-51; 25:30)?

21. According to the context, what kingdom is in view in Matthew 6:10?

22. Is Matthew 6:14-15 to be reconciled with Ephesians 4:32; Colossians 3:13; 1 John 1:9?

In his article on "Modern Dispensationalism" (Evangelical Quarterly, Vol. VIII, No. 1) already cited, Dr. Allis objects to the notes in the Scofield Reference Bible bearing on the fifth petition of the Lord's Prayer. The specific note in question reads as follows: "This is legal ground. Cf. Eph. 4:32, which is grace. Under law forgiveness is conditioned upon a like spirit in us; under grace we are forgiven for Christ's sake, and exhorted to forgive because we have been forgiven. See Matt. 18:32; 26:28 note." Similarly, Dr. Allis objects to Dr. Scofield's citation of Matthew 18:32-33 and Ephesians 4:32 together as Dr. Scofield does in his summary on forgiveness (p. 1038), when pointing out the principle of human forgiveness.

Dr. Allis objects to the use of Matthew 18:32-33 to represent grace since the context goes on to say: "So likewise shall my heavenly Father do also unto you, if ye from your hearts forgive not every one his brother their trespasses." In making this criticism it appears that Dr. Allis has overlooked the fact that Dr. Scofield is here discussing the principle of human forgiveness as in contrast to divine forgiveness. Human forgiveness, quite apart from divine grace, is man's forgiveness of his fellow man, and Dr. Scofield points out that human forgiveness rests upon and results from divine forgiveness, that is, the normal impulse in a human heart to forgive comes from the recognition that one has been forgiven. It matters nothing to this human motive whether God has forgiven because we forgive, as in Matthew 6:14-15, or for Christ's sake, as in Ephesians 4:32. The motivating principle in human forgiveness is the same in either case. Ephesians 4:32 and Colossians 2:13 present a forgiveness which rests on no human merit whatever, and apparently refer primarily to the once-for-all forgiveness which belongs to salvation by grace. In 1 John 1:9, where household forgiveness is in view, there is the one and most essential condition of confession set up for the child of God; but grace relationships, whether for salvation, as in Ephesians 4:32 and Colossians 2:13, or for restoration, as in 1 John 1:9, do not introduce the element of merit which element is found in Matthew 6:14-15 and 18:34-35.

The one who contends that the meritorious principle in forgiveness, which is presented in Matthew 6:14-15 and 18:34-35, applies to the Christian imposes on himself and others the conception of God that He is not propitious until rendered so by the human acts of forgiveness; that He is "wroth"; and that He will deliver His own redeemed ones who are in Christ to the "tormentors" until they make legal and equitable payment to Him for every offense. Is any Christian now believing that he has no more divine forgiveness than he merits by the exercise of human forgiveness? But one other step, which is taught by some, need be added to this, namely, that the Christian, following the supposed divine pattern, should not forgive his enemies until they are penitent. Thus it would be arranged that God forgives only when the Christian forgives, but the Christian cannot forgive until his enemies are penitent; the conclusion being that the Christian cannot be forgiven until his enemies are penitent.

All such conclusions are foreign to the revelation that Christ is the propitiation for our sins. Dr. Allis does not and could not demonstrate that Matthew 6:14-15 and Ephesians 4:32 represent similar principles in divine forgiveness. Thus the real issue which Dr. Scofield is presenting is left without an argument against it. Dr. Allis does quote from the Westminster Shorter Catechism in support of his contention that Matthew 6:14-15, which must include 18:34-35, is applicable to Christians under grace. The Catechism states: "In the fifth petition ... we pray, that God, for Christ's sake, would fully pardon all our sins, which we are rather encouraged to ask, because by his grace we are enabled from the heart to forgive others." As a comment on this quotation, it may be observed that the Catechism, no matter how much it is revered, has no authority to insert into the Lord's Prayer the phrase for Christ's sake.

The new and limitless privilege of prayer in the name of Christ or for Christ's sake was not extended until in the Upper Room when Christ was anticipating the new relationship under grace. In the Upper Room Discourse He said, regarding the new ground of prayer, "Hitherto have ye asked nothing in my name" (John 16:24). This includes every previous prayer the disciples had ever prayed ·· not excepting the Lord's Prayer. It is therefore not the prerogative of the Catechism to put this petition into the Lord's Prayer when Christ distinctly declares that it could not belong there. It is this assumed freedom to soften the elements of law with grace and to vitiate grace with law which leads to confusion and which blinds good men to the most imperative and vital distinctions in the Word of God.

In pursuing this same general criticism of Dr. Scofield's notes, Dr. Allis quotes Schaff, with apparent approval, as follows: "The typical catechisms of Protestantism ... are essentially agreed. ... They teach the articles of the Apostles' Creed, the Ten Commandments, and the Lord's Prayer; that is all that is necessary for a man to believe and to do in order to be saved." We might inquire what plan of salvation these brethren discover in the Lord's Prayer and the Ten Commandments? The Apostles' Creed does include a statement of belief in historic facts related to Christ, but no word is found there of personal appropriation of the value of those facts. This essential element is seen in Paul's testimony: "He loved me, and gave himself for me." An inquiry is in order, again, concerning how many lost souls have been led to a saving knowledge of a crucified and risen Savior by the Lord's Prayer, the Ten Commandments, and the Apostles' Creed. And do these articles contain that gospel which the Apostle Paul declared was specifically revealed unto him?

In another article Dr. Allis asks whether the author of this thesis teaches his students not to pray the so-called Lord's Prayer. In reply, it is asked whether Dr. Allis teaches that one should pray the prayer of Matthew 24:20. It will be seen that Christ directs the praying of one prayer as much as He does the other.

Chapter V
Conclusion

Chapter V
Conclusion

The 22 questions concluding Chapter IV with the problems they develop might be multiplied many times and extended to all parts of the Sacred Text. Dispensationalists do not create these problems nor do they invent the right divisions of Scripture. For the dispensationalist, these so-called problems are not only solved but, because of the distinctions which the problems demand, the problems become a part of the overwhelming evidence that his method of interpretation is according to truth. Those who pursue an idealism regarding the unity and continuity of the Bible, which idealism is built upon and sustained only by occasional or accidental similarities, must, if sincere, face the problems their method of interpretation generates.

The limited array of evidence about God's specific purposes which this thesis presents is sufficient to demonstrate that dispensationalism, even though it does recognize the divine age-purposes and does departmentalize the message of the Word of God according to its obvious divisions, does also discover the true unity and continuity of the Bible. The outstanding characteristic of the dispensationalist is the fact that he believes every statement of the Bible and gives to it the plain, natural meaning its words imply. This simple plan has changed the Bible from being a mass of more or less conflicting writings into a classified and easily assimilated revelation of both the earthly and heavenly purposes of God, which purposes reach on into eternity to come. He is saved from working at cross purposes with God, and the exposition he gives of the Scriptures, like the uncompromised gospel he preaches, is blessed to the multitudes who are attracted by his understandable message.

There is a reason why churches are filled, souls are saved, and the interest in missionary work thrives, where the whole Bible with its vital distinctions is faithfully preached. Agreement cannot be accorded to recent writers who accuse the faithful Bible expositors and evangelists of this and past generations of being modernists, and only because they stand for that form of doctrine and recognize those distinctions which are invariably discovered when the whole Bible is considered and believed and when it is given its plain and reasonable interpretation. The situation which necessitates the writing of this thesis serves to demonstrate the wide doctrinal differences that may exist between supposedly orthodox men. A crisis is evidently being reached concerning the issues which have long separated expositors from theological theorists, and this distinction does not imply that the expositor does not know Systematic Theology, for usually he does know it well; however, he builds his theology directly upon the Word of God and is in no bondage to the opinions of men.

At the beginning of this thesis it was stated that the doctrinal differences herein discussed are due to the fact that the two schools of interpretation involved stand on widely divergent premises. The dispensationalist believes that throughout the ages God is pursuing two distinct purposes: one related to the earth with earthly people and earthly objectives involved, which is Judaism; while the other is related to heaven with heavenly people and heavenly objectives involved, which is Christianity. Why should this belief be deemed so incredible in the light of the facts that there is a present distinction between earth and heaven which is preserved even after both are made new; when the Scriptures so designate an earthly people who go on as such into eternity; and a heavenly people who also abide in their heavenly calling forever? Over against this, the partial dispensationalist, though dimly observing a few obvious distinctions, bases his interpretation on the supposition that God is doing but one thing, namely, the general separation of the good from the bad, and, in spite of all the confusion this limited theory creates, contends that the earthly people merge into the heavenly people; that the earthly program must be given a spiritual interpretation or disregarded altogether.

The advocates of this interpretation oppose every earthly feature of the divine program. They disregard or ignore the earthly covenants and promises; they spiritualize or vaporize the vast body of Scripture bearing on the Davidic throne and kingdom; they present no specific reason why Christ was born as the Son of David; and they recognize no earthly glory or purpose in His second advent. According to their system, Christ comes again to end the world, but, unfortunately for these conceptions, the world does not end then or ever.

May the number, already vast indeed, of those who believe the Bible and are subject to its plain teachings continue to increase!

The End

Made in the USA
San Bernardino, CA
12 January 2017